STAR WARS
INSIDER

THE GALAXY'S GREATEST HEROES

WWW.TITAN-COMICS.COM

Star Wars Insider:
The Galaxy's Greatest Heroes

ISBN: 9781787736368

Published by Titan
A division of
Titan Publishing Group Ltd.,
144 Southwark Street,
London, SE1 0UP

© 2021 Lucasfilm Ltd. and ™
All Rights Reserved.
Used Under Authorised User.

No part of this publication may be reproduced, stored in a retrieval system, or transmitted, in any form or by any means, without the prior written permission of the publisher.

A CIP catalogue record for this title is available from the British Library.

First Edition November 2021
10 9 8 7 6 5 4 3 2 1

Printed in China.

Acknowledgments
Titan would like to thank the cast and crews of the *Star Wars* saga. A huge thanks also to Brett Rector and Michael Siglain at Lucasfilm, and Eugene Paraszczuk, Kevin Pearl, and Christopher Troise at Disney for all of their invaluable help in putting this volume together.

THE GALAXY'S GREATEST HEROES

CONTENTS

006   LUKE SKYWALKER

024   PRINCESS LEIA

040   HAN SOLO AND CHEWBACCA

056   OBI-WAN KENOBI

074   AHSOKA TANO

088   YODA

104   LANDO CALRISSIAN

112   PADMÉ AMIDALA

126   C-3PO AND R2-D2

136   REY

148   FINN

156   JYN ERSO

164   POE DAMERON

170   WICKET

LUKE SKYWALKER

LUKE SKYWALKER

A farm boy who fulfilled his destiny to become a Jedi Knight, Luke Skywalker's journey was an echo of the actor who played him, Mark Hamill.

A relative newcomer when he successfully auditioned for the role of Luke Skywalker for what was then George Lucas' *The Star Wars*, Californian born Mark Hamill was catapulated into fame, becoming an instant icon as the farm boy-turned-warrior.

Mark Hamill (Luke Skywalker): Can you imagine sitting down to read the screenplay to what was then called, *The Adventures of Luke Starkiller, as taken from 'The Journal of the Whills,' Saga I: The Star Wars*? I thought, *Boy, they have to work on this title*. I started reading the script and I couldn't believe my eyes.

I thought, *This thing is hilarious!* Most science fiction is very dry, but the dialogue in *Star Wars* is so funny. This idea of robots arguing over whose fault it is... [*Hamill performs a flawless C-3PO impersonation*]: "I've forgotten how much I abhor space travel!" I was just falling out of my chair laughing! The robots are so human and warm.

I also loved the character of Han Solo. I thought it was so smart to have a cynical, modern day voice mocking the Force. He really doesn't care one way or the other: he's in it for the money. I thought, *That's really going to draw a lot of people in who would resist this kind of material, because they'll completely identify with him*. I knew Harrison Ford's work from *American Graffiti* (1973). I thought, *Oh, this guy's just going to knock it out of the ballpark*—and of course, he did!

There's also a spirituality there that was unusual for science fiction. They were talking about this entity that's bigger than all of us, that links us together. It was pretty heavy stuff for the kind of Saturday matinée, fun serial, which it was emulating.

While Hamill had enjoyed the script, his faith in the material was not always shared by others.

Mark Hamill: I predicted that *Star Wars* would be bigger than *Planet of the Apes* (1968), and I mean the one with Charlton Heston. Even if it tanked at the box office, it has 'cult classic' written all over it. It seems to me that most science fiction was so serious up until that time. I said it's like *The Little Rascals* (1955) in outer space. It has its serious side, no question about it. It was wonderful the way they used the Force to appeal to people's spirituality without making them uncomfortable by talking about religion. You have a farm boy, a princess, a cynical space pirate, and a wizard. To me, it is much more like fairy tales and fables than it is science fiction. If we were traveling in horse-drawn carriages, it could be set in medieval times.

An avid comic book fan, Hamill's love of popular culture, including comics and movies, ensured that he understood the genre of George Lucas' script.

▶

LUKE SKYWALKER

1 / Mark Hamill as Luke Skywalker in a publicity shot for *Star Wars: The Empire Strikes Back* (1980). (Previous spread)

2 / Hamill on location in Tunisia for *Star Wars: A New Hope* (1977).

3 / Luke meets the droids.

4 / Luke watches the Empire's fight against the rebels in a scene excised from the final cut of the film.

5 / Sharing a lighter moment wih the droids and co-star Sir Alec Guinness.

6 / Luke Skywalker illustrated by the artist of the *Star Wars* comic book, Howard Chaykin.

7 / George Lucas with his actors on location. (Next spread).

▶ **Mark Hamill:** My father was in the Navy so we moved from coast to coast. Maybe what I needed was attention. The first things that I remember loving were the comic strips that came to my doorstep every day. I learned to read from [those] strips. I loved to draw and idolized [*Peanuts* creator] Charles M. Schulz.

Later, I loved the Universal horror films that were, of course, banned in our house. I was told, "You're not seeing that stuff," and that just made me want to watch even more. You might as well buy me the ticket and drive me to the theater when you say that. I learned that as a parent; you can't be too strict.

I loved *Frankenstein* (1931) with Boris Karloff, *The Wolf Man* (1941), Bela Lugosi as *Dracula* (1931), and Christopher Lee and Peter Cushing in the Hammer films. The original version of *King Kong* (1933) is probably still my all-time favorite movie.

The young Hamill spent his time building model kits of movie creatures and studied the *Famous Monsters of Filmland* magazine for behind-the-scenes secrets.

Mark Hamill: The issue of *Famous Monsters* that explained how they did the stop-motion animation for *King Kong* was fascinating to me. I wanted to let it be magic, yet I couldn't stop reading how it was done. I have reservations about making-of documentaries because I like [movies] to be magical. When you see how they are filmed, it's like a magician revealing his greatest secrets. You want to know but when you learn, it's always kind of disappointing.

10 | STAR WARS: THE GALAXY'S GREATEST HEROES

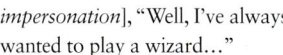

LUKE SKYWALKER

impersonation], "Well, I've always wanted to play a wizard…"

He saw—very much like I did—that it was more like a fairy tale than traditional science fiction. Science fiction tends to be a projection of what life will be in the future from the point of view of Earthlings—and fantasy can be anything! There's a big furry ape-like creature flying your spaceship, wearing headphones, not wearing any pants? Sure, why not? It's fantasy!

The films combine elements of so many wonderful things: from the Ray Harryhausen films, to *The Wizard of Oz* (1939), to *Captain Blood* (1935), to *The Searchers* (1956). It's a movie-lover's dream to work in something that plays on so many elements that make cinema unique.

While Hamill loved the script, and was excited to be working with his co-stars, the process of shooting the film was less than ideal.

Mark Hamill: We were always reminded that it was a children's film. The British crew could only relate it to something like *Doctor Who* (1963-onwards) or *Dan Dare* (1950-onwards) or the more idiosyncratic British things they'd done. They were sure that it would only play at matinées for

Being a fan of classic cinema, the actor was delighted to work with Sir Alec Guinness, one of his acting idols.

Mark Hamill: My Mom was a huge Alec Guinness fan. She took me to see *The Ladykillers* (1955), *The Lavender Hill Mob* (1951), and *The Horse's Mouth* (1958). When I found out that both Alec Guinness and Peter Cushing were going to be in *Star Wars*, I was just beside myself. I remember reading the script and thinking, *Darn, I'm not in a scene with Peter Cushing!*

I got a chance to get to know Alec Guinness and I asked him outright, "Why did you want to do this?" He was so legendary in his accomplishments, and I was so flattered to be in something that he thought was worthy for his résumé! He said to me [*Hamill performs a perfect Sir Alec Guinness*

STAR WARS: THE GALAXY'S GREATEST HEROES | 11

LUKE SKYWALKER

kids at weekends. I wasn't insulted by that at all! I thought, They could be right! What appealed to me was it was also meant for the kid in all of us, much like the Disney films are. You can be moved by *Bambi* (1942) or delighted by *Pinocchio* (1940) no matter what your age is. It seemed to me that it had great potential.

Less confident was Hamill's director, George Lucas, who was watching his vision slowly unravel as the demands of filming took their toll.

Mark Hamill: George isn't the happiest guy when he's directing. In fact he seems sort of morose and depressed! It must be hard because he'd imagined *Star Wars* for so many years and then when you see it realized in a literal sense on set, he was disappointed. "This is a lightsaber? It doesn't look so hot!"

Sometimes robots don't exactly behave in the way you want them to—not Anthony Daniels, of course—but the mechanical ones that were meant to do this and that! We really had to move along. George called it "the most expensive low-budget movie ever made," because we didn't have the luxury of infinite takes or expanding our schedule. It was dodgy for a while. I was on a need-to-know basis, but I learned later that they screened it for Fox executives and George's film buddies with no score—I think they used classical pieces from *The Planets* to stand in for what would become John Williams' score. But [Fox Vice President of Creative Affairs] Alan Ladd and the powers-that-be saw the potential.

Despite others wavering, Hamill never quite lost faith.

Mark Hamill: I'd signed a contract that if the first one was successful, that it would be a trilogy, with a beginning,

8 /

9 /

a middle, and an end. I was confident, because I realized that even if *Star Wars* stumbled at the box office, it will get the reputation of a cult movie, like *The Rocky Horror Picture Show* (1975). It'll be embraced by a small fan base, and there'll be midnight showings.

Since the original *Star Wars* movie only cost about $9 million, I figured if we made $25 million, it would break even. I looked at all the grosses for fantasy and science fiction films since the start of the talkies. I said, "I bet this thing could make upwards of $50 million!" I had no idea we'd be on the cover of *Time* magazine! During filming I asked George how long it was going to be. He said, "Hmmm, maybe an hour and 57 minutes." That was just like George to say something that specific! He said, "Anything over two-hours is an epic!" His thinking has changed over the years, obviously, but he's had a lot more story to tell. It was never lost on me—that anything over two hours is an epic, and that should give you some idea of at least the approach that we had in those days. You may be an epic, but don't act like one. Be true to the material, don't be pretentious ▶

8 / Hamill flanked by Phil Brown (Uncle Owen) and George Lucas.

9 / Taking a moment behind the camera.

10 / Hamill poses for an early publicity shot.

10 / Production art by Ralph McQuarrie showing Luke facing down against an AT-AT, a scene that would have signifcance for Hamill. (Next spread).

LUKE SKYWALKER

and don't be pompous. It was the only way we could do it, because it wasn't a foregone conclusion that so many people would have such reverence for it. It was very loose and ragged around the edges, which I think works well in contrast to the spectacular special effects. I like that kind of knockabout feel that we had.

Obviously, as it went on we had bigger budgets and the special effects get more and more accomplished. Each movie has a different sort of atmosphere and tone, but we never forgot where we came from.

12 / Taking a look through the lens on the set of The Empire Strikes Back.

13 / Luke, after barely surviving an encounter with a rancor in Star Wars: Return of the Jedi.

14 / Hamill takes a moment to relax on set with his only co-star for weeks: Yoda!

With *Star Wars*—soon to have the subtitle *A New Hope* attached—a hit earning well-beyond *Planet of the Apes* numbers, the actor started preparations for the sequel. To get himself ready for the lightsaber dueling scenes in *The Empire Strikes Back*, Hamill endured a training regimen comprised of fencing, gymnastics, and martial arts.

Mark Hamill: *The Empire Strikes Back* was the most physically challenging of the three [films]. It's like going to work and being beaten up for twelve hours. I would come home with bruises on my body that looked like a relief map of Venezuela. Bob Anderson, an Olympic fencing champion, was doing the sword fighting for David [Prowse]. He made me look much better than I was. You learn the routine as if it were choreographed. When you make mistakes, somebody that skilled can make your mistakes look purposeful.

Hamill, and his wife Marilou have a very special memory of the filming of *Empire*: the birth of their first son, Nathan.

Mark Hamill: We were [staying] at the house where A. A. Milne wrote *Winnie-the-Pooh* (1921). This was also the place where we lost Brian Jones of The Rolling Stones, so it had great historical significance. Marilou went into labor and I escorted her to the hospital. Nathan was born in the wee small hours. Both mother and child were healthy and fine but in need of a good rest.

I went to the house for a nap and planned to return to the hospital in the morning then I get a phone call saying, "Mark, we just need one shot from you today."

Hamill, a team player even on his day off, went in to shoot a fateful scene of Luke attacking an AT-AT.

Mark Hamill: They said, "Run toward the camera, look over your shoulder, get a shot off with your gun, and jump as far as you can." A boom microphone operator said, "I'm surprised we brought you in for a 'gorilla smoking a pipe' shot." I was certain that I had misheard the operator, and asked him for an explanation. "When you've got the jumpsuit on and the

car in the studio and the crew is rocking the vehicle to make it look like there's movement, and they're running lights past my face. How is that any different? It's so unlike really driving a car! And that's not that much different to doing something like being in the cockpit of the *Millennium Falcon* and having them rock that. It's all about pretend. I used to play in the backyard as Zorro or Robin Hood or Sinbad battling skeletons in my mind. That was all the stuff I loved. To this day, I'm so grateful for all those things that I really loved as a child—whether it's comic books, or movies, or television, or comic strips, or puppets.

Hamill had many scenes that featured just Luke and the Jedi Master Yoda, realized on screen by the puppeteer and voice performer Frank Oz.

Mark Hamill: After Carrison (that's what I called Harrison Ford and Carrie Fisher) went back to the United States after finishing their scenes, I was the only human being on the call sheet for weeks! It was me, snakes, robots, and a puppet. It got very lonely because Frank, Wendy [Midener], and all

helmet with goggles on and you're about the size of your thumb on a big, wide frame, then it could be anybody in that shot; it could be a gorilla smoking a pipe."

I did the shot like they told me and jumped as far as I could toward the camera. When I landed, I sprained my thumb. Because of the injury, I couldn't hold a lightsaber properly and many of the dueling scenes were postponed for several weeks until my thumb healed.

The demands of the story meant that Hamill had to make imaginative leaps in order to work with the special effects that would be later added into shots.

Mark Hamill: Pretend is pretend; I had an overall view of what it looked like in my imagination. People ask, "Was it hard being in something like that where nothing's there or you're working with greenscreen?" Well, I do movies where I'm supposed to be driving a car, and it's a cutaway

15 /

the Yoda operators were below the set. I had an earpiece so that I could hear Frank, but it was not really like being with him. I'd see him at lunch and in the little room where they would run off to repair Yoda when he broke down. Whenever you see me by myself, I'm not looking at Yoda off-camera. I'm looking at a stick with a piece of tape on it for an eyeline. There were so many problems because there was movement in his ears, and mechanical movement in his eyes. There were problems with Yoda breaking down or looking cross-eyed or the ears not working.

I adored Yoda. Frank is just so instrumental in that character being what he is—manipulating the figure itself and providing the voice. I remember someone saying, "Does he sound too much like Grover from *Sesame Street*?" And I thought *No, you can't change that voice: It's got to be Frank!* I never had to make any sort of leap into believing in Yoda. We went on a weekend to rehearse on a non-shooting day, and Frank had to get used to this puppet that [makeup artist] Stuart Freeborn had built with the help from Jim Henson's team. It was the first

16 /

15 / Luke's anger gets the better of him in *Return of the Jedi*.

16 / Signing autographs for fans in the Yuma desert location where Luke's daring rescue of his friends from Jabba the Hutt was filmed.

time we were actually doing scenes together. I'm telling you, the minute he put his hand inside that face, Frank melted away, and to me he was Yoda.

Frank was always very complimentary to me. He said, "Well, if you didn't believe it, then nobody else would believe it." But he was just being modest because Yoda wasn't a puppet—he was a real, breathing character. But I think ignorance is bliss, because it didn't occur to me that anybody else wouldn't believe in Yoda either, even though it should have—he was walking like a Muppet, you never saw his feet! One of the most brilliant things is when you see him put one knee up on a box as he's about to climb up, and it cuts to me saying, "Will you get out of there?", not knowing that he's this great Jedi warrior and thinking he's just some eccentric little amphibian. The audience sees that knee go up and the suggestion of his feet is enough so that they fill it in for themselves. That was the only

LUKE SKYWALKER

thing I was worried about—that you can't really show him below the waist. It's the combination of the artistry of Frank Oz and the writing of Lawrence Kasdan [and George Lucas]—all of it worked.

Following the release of Return of the Jedi in 1983, Hamill felt it was perhaps time to take the advice Obi-Wan gave to Luke in A New Hope and "let go."

Mark Hamill: At some point I figured, "I've got to let it go!" Especially when George made the prequels. I didn't know he was going to wait so long to do them! I was drawn to wanting to visit the set, but I thought I should hold back because it should be a fresh start. It should stand on its own. If the roles were reversed, I wouldn't want somebody saying, "Well, in my day we did X, Y, Z." I didn't want people to think I was trying to give advice or anything. But I did get a really nice telegram from Frank Oz on the very first day of Episode I saying, "It won't be the same without you."

Luke's journey continued in the sequel trilogy of films, starting with an appearance during the conclusion of Star Wars: The Force Awakens (2015), leading to a continuation and culmination of Luke's story in Star Wars: The Last Jedi (2017) and Star Wars: The Rise of Skywalker (2019).

Mark Hamill: I never in a million years expected to be back. I thought if they did a third trilogy, it would be set ten, fifty, or even one hundred years in the future, so it was completely unexpected. I enjoyed it in a way I never could have in my twenties.

The film took some unexpected twists and turns with Luke becoming a recluse, far, far away from the galactic turmoil caused by the resurgent First Order.

Mark Hamill: At some point, people doubt Luke is a real person. Because of the gravity of the situation, the urgency of the situation, Rey doesn't have the luxury of getting to know him and relax and exchange ideas. She needs him and wants to enlist his help and abilities to her cause. And that's the conflict. Luke's in a very different place than we've ever seen him before. Luke always represented hope and optimism. And now, here he is, pessimistic, disillusioned, and demoralized.

17 / Luke Skywalker is brought before Darth Vader on Endor.

LUKE SKYWALKER

> "*Star Wars* is so optimistic and inspiring. It encourages you to do the right thing, and to not think of yourself."

▶ There's no one more deserving of trust [than Rian Johnson]. If you look at his movies, each is different than the last. You can't pigeonhole him and say, "That's the kind of film he makes." *The Last Jedi* is so different in many, subtle ways, than the other *Star Wars* movies, and yet it is really satisfying in delivering what the fans want to see as well.

During a key moment in the film, Hamill stepped onto the *Millennium Falcon* set, bringing back memories going back over 40 years.

Mark Hamill: It's like going to your old high school or the house you lived in in sixth grade. The detail was perfect. It was just as I remembered it. I climbed up and down the ladder, got in the hold where we stowed away, and sat in the cockpit with my grown children and wife. Later I slipped away and got really choked up. It really was a special moment.

Being the headline guest at the popular *Star Wars* Celebration conventions, has cemented the actors' performance as Luke as a pop culture icon.

Mark Hamill: Appearing at Celebration is almost like what it must have been like in The Beatles or, more appropriately, The Monkees. Our experience was being chosen by George, rather than organically forming a group like The Beatles. Mickey Dolenz and I will be on lunchboxes as long as we live! We're part of that little niche pop-culture experience that has brought so many people so much pleasure long after we thought it would be all finished.

It truly is an amazing accomplishment for George Lucas to have created something that has endured and will continue to endure. It's like L. Frank Baum with the *Oz* books, J.R.R. Tolkien with *The Lord of the Rings*, and Gene Roddenberry with *Star Trek*. As long as people have imaginations and the desire to dream and want to enjoy entertainment that takes them out of their everyday lives, then *Star Wars* will never die.

Star Wars is so optimistic, and inspiring. It encourages you to do the right thing, and to not think of yourself, but rather to do what's right for the greater good.

People say, "You're so associated with that one thing that you can't be thought of in any other way." I guess there are elements to that, but they're so outweighed by the positives. ☮

18 / Luke faces a new challenge when Rey arrives to disrupt his hermitage.

19 / Luke Skywalker on Ahch-To.

LEIA ORGANA

LEIA ORGANA

A devastating combination of beauty, wit, and steely determination, Leia Organa is every bit as iconic as the woman who portrayed her in six feature films, Carrie Fisher.

A groundbreaking female lead, Carrie Fisher's performance as an atypical princess who gave as good as she got led to her being an enduring fan favorite. The daughter of Hollywood megastars Eddie Fisher and Debbie Reynolds, it was perhaps inevitable that Fisher would become an actress.

Carrie Fisher (Leia Organa): When I was in 6th grade, I did my first play. I played a squaw in the 7th grade production—it was really big stuff! I was the big kid on campus that year. And I used to take musical comedy courses. I always liked it; it was like recess to me. And it was a way of getting out of school, too.

Fisher enjoyed playing the sassy princess who rescued her rescuers while criticizing their efforts.

Carrie Fisher: George Lucas was groundbreaking in creating Leia. People keep telling me he was. I have people come up to me and say that my character inspired them to live their lives the way they did. There was a playful side that people got out of it, and there was the side of it where you think of yourself as being capable. The Princess is someone who takes responsibility for her life and makes choices and has a life. She doesn't fall into things. Over the years nothing has changed, except the hair.

Still in her teens when cast as Leia, Fisher had recently attended drama school in England where she would film her scenes for *Star Wars*.

Carrie Fisher: I grew up in the *Star Wars* saga. While everyone else was 25 to 30, I was only 19 when the filming started. You can see me growing in each new episode. I used to kid everyone on the set by saying that I had an excuse—I was a teenager, but why were all these grown-ups shooting guns, and playing with all the big toys? I almost think I looked totally different when we did *Return of the Jedi*.

I was cast as Leia Organa in *Star Wars* straight from an English drama school. Quite a jump! Leia is a royal and is angry, which is part of her strength but not all of it. She is very clear about her responsibilities toward her cause, the Rebellion, and that was it for her. That commitment didn't leave her any time for relationships. While it was OK for "the boys" to be strong, that same strength made Leia seem, somehow, almost mean or sarcastic with her "my way or no way" attitude.

Basically, Leia was the only female in the original *Star Wars* trilogy. Oh, there's Aunt Beru, and some characters in *Return of the Jedi*, but Leia remains the main female role. Originally I was known as "the girl." During my first day on the set, someone described the next scene I was in ▶

2 /

1 / Carrie Fisher as Leia Organa in a publicity shot for Star Wars: The Empire Strikes Back. (Previous spread)

2 / Luke, Leia and Han Solo: the heroes of Star Wars: A New Hope.

3 / A tense moment for the princess during the climax of A New Hope.

4 / George Lucas directs Peter Cushing and Fisher on the Death Star set.

5 / Behind-the-scenes with Mark Hamill, Anthony Daniels, Kenny Baker, Carrie Fisher, and a nearly out of shot Harrison Ford! (Next spread)

as, "the girl crosses the room and exits stage left. The camera operator will have to pan to keep her in frame." I asked whether I was to be "the girl" or "the camera operator." They got the idea and I'm now an honorary camera operator!

The actress was aware of differences between each film of the original trilogy.

Carrie Fisher: Each film in the original trilogy is unique! Each had its own director with his own different way of working, and it was lovely having a chance to work with all of them, yet there is still that thread of continuity. A New Hope was an introduction to the characters.

The Empire Strikes Back really developed the relationships of the main characters. You got to know them a little better. Our director, Irvin Kershner, required that everything in a scene "work" beforehand, so reshooting a particular scene wouldn't just be a matter of redoing the same scene faster. Kersh was always willing to talk over any little bit of a scene to make it more comfortable for the actors.

I liked the script for Return of the Jedi. Leia's character undergoes quite a change. They found a way for her to be nice while remaining strong and committed. Leia is quite feminine. Her character is as clearly defined as the boys, and she even dresses "like a woman." It's been nice having the chance to work on a character that developed throughout the movies.

Return of the Jedi was a very complex movie with a lot of scenes that had to be done in front of a

4 /

26 | STAR WARS: THE GALAXY'S GREATEST HEROES

LEIA ORGANA

blue screen, where the actors would only have Richard Marquand's [director] verbal description to establish what is supposed to be going on. There are so many things to consider, and it takes a lot to get every detail right. You have to get the acting just right, the droids moving right. You even have to take off the creature's heads so the actors don't faint from the heat. The work can be a bit trying, but it's a lot of fun to do. It was a great crew, we were like a family.

Fisher found herself charmed by the adulation she received for her role as Leia.

Carrie Fisher: After the first *Star Wars* movie, I would get love letters from nine-year-old boys who would compare me to "a summer's day." It was very sweet of them. They sent such lovely letters. Much of my mail was from children, and some grown-ups, who had seen the movie 50 times each. I like the fans. I always looked forward to those letters.

Fisher was also the center of attention from her co-stars.

Mark Hamill: As actors, you are paid to really relate to whatever [the part] is. It isn't surprising that people fall in love with their co-stars and these affairs happen and marriages break up. It's a blurry line and you really start believing it. Harrison and I would try to get Carrie's attention, not so much to make Carrie our girlfriend, but just to be cool around her or be funnier than the other guy. You can imagine my shock when I found out our status as siblings in the movie! It's like

STAR WARS: THE GALAXY'S GREATEST HEROES | 27

LEIA ORGANA

▶ one of those "good news, bad news" jokes. The good news is that there is an attractive woman in this universe; the bad news is that she's your sister. I can remember asking George Lucas, "Where are all the other women in this universe?"

Her human costars were the least of her problems. A certain Kowakian Monkey-Lizard also took a shine to the princess.

Tim Rose (Salacious B. Crumb): When we were filming the Jabba's Palace scenes I was a young man, and like most young men at the time I had a very strong attraction to Carrie Fisher in her metal bikini! Unlike most young men, I got to be very close to her for hours at a time. In between, takes my character, Salacious B. Crumb, used to pretend he was Gomez Addams and Carrie was Morticia from the TV series *The Addams Family* (1964-1965). He would start at her ankle, and slowly kiss his way up her calf saying,"Oh Cara Mia! I am defenceless against your beauty." Then they would call, "Turn over," and we would have to go to work. She was always amused by Salacious's antics, but I couldn't help but feel if I had tried anything like that myself I would have been forcibly removed from the production. As we learned performing as The Muppets: Puppets can get away with murder!

For many years it seemed that *Return of the Jedi* would be Fisher's final performance as Leia. But with the Disney Corporation's acquisition of Lucasfilm, the actress was called into service again—at a *Star Wars* fan convention!

Carrie Fisher: We were at *Star Wars* Celebration. We were brought into a room and were seated at a long table, like we were having a meeting about the shareholders. Then, it wasn't about that... ▶

6 / Fisher enjoys a lighter moment on set with Anthony Daniels (C-3PO).

7 / A pensive Leia aboard the *Millennium Falcon*.

8 / Carrie Fisher on the set of *The Empire Strikes Back*.

9 /

9 / The Empire catches up with Leia in this publicity shot for *The Empire Strikes Back*.

10 / Fisher is joined by Mark Hamill and producer Gary Kurtz during the filming of the final scene of *The Empire Strikes Back*.

11/ The princess rescues Han Solo from his carbonite prison in *Return of the Jedi*.

▶ The new trilogy of films would reunite the cast of the original trilogy for the first time in over 30 years, with the first installment directed by J.J. Abrams.

Carrie Fisher: What I felt like with J.J. Abrams is that he loved these films. It's not part of your history; it's part of your childhood. Little kids grew up watching this, and J.J. is one of those. And there's a tremendous responsibility to this thing that he treasured. He was taking that seriously. He was excited by it. There's responsibility that goes with that, and he seemed completely up for that. J.J. is someone who's proven he can do these epic, otherworldly films, and also worldly films. He's a writer and a director and he loves movies. That really comes across.

Fisher, had one stipulation that wasn't met in the final cut.

Carrie Fisher: I wanted to use the iconic hairstyle that I had initially. I wanted that hairstyle back. If nothing else, I wanted little old Leia to walk by a window wearing that hairdo on the way to the bathtub. Just show it once. But no, I guess they thought it would be too distracting.

Fisher was delighted to be working with an extraordinary cast of familar and less well-known co-stars.

Carrie Fisher: I was nervous and excited. We had a good time together. Everyone was nervous in different ways. Watching Daisy Ridley, she has grown enormously through the process of filming. She's very confident, very at ease. So, it's definitely a home to her. John always seemed comfortable. John came into the situation very confident, ready to get at it.

It was really good to have the original cast back. It was like a *Star Wars* high school reunion. Anthony Daniels looked exactly the same!

The Force Awakens also introduced Leia's son, Ben Solo aka Kylo Ren.

Carrie Fisher: Playing a villain, you don't know you're a villain. This is your cause, and this is what Adam is doing. He's passionate, but he's also solitary.

Fisher had a clear view as to what she, and her fellow returning cast-members brought to the set.

Carrie Fisher: We've moved on. So you have more experience to bring to what you're looking at; to bring to bear upon the situation. You were an innocent; you were moving faster when you were a kid when you were making these films. So, now we're looking at it with a lot more experience.

With worldwide anticipation for *The Force Awakens* reaching fever pitch, Fisher was all too aware of what the *Star Wars* saga means to the saga's millions of enthusiasts.

LEIA ORGANA

Carrie Fisher: This is [the fans'] fairytale. This is what they grew up with, what their fantasies were propelled by. It was this other world. They belong to that other world and they feel a part of that. They feel like they know you and to an extent they do. The funniest thing to me, and the sweetest thing to me, is when they bring you a three-week-old child wearing the Leia outfit. It's also seeing these tiny kids and the children know who you are. That's the oddest, sweetest, most fascinating aspect of it. I think the fans were happy to be in their home away from home again.

One such fan found himself working on the same film as his childhood idol.

Simon Pegg (Unkar Plutt): I once lined up at in Comic-Con International: San Diego in 2004 when I was there to promote *Shaun of the Dead*. I finished a signing on the floor and stood up, walked out of my booth and joined the line to meet Carrie Fisher. I waited for an hour and then finally got to her and told her that I had a picture of her by my bedside on the wall that I would kiss every night before I went to sleep. She was my first crush. She said to me, "Do you feel better for telling me that?" And I said, "Yes, thank you very much," and I walked off with her autograph.

Years later, I was on set and Carrie and I were having a conversation. We were walking around set, chatting together and I said, "I lined up to meet you once." And then a couple weeks ago, I asked her to marry me, which was really nice. But she checked my finger. I should have taken the ring off.

The excitement for seeing the original cast reunited extended to their colleagues.

STAR WARS: THE GALAXY'S GREATEST HEROES | 33

12 /

Oscar Isaac: When you see Carrie, and Harrison Ford, C-3PO and R2-D2 and Chewbacca. These are icons in the flesh. That's when you get a little bit of chills like, *Wow, this is actually happening!* They've been great, particularly Carrie, who's so funny. I find her to be very kind and it's been a lot of fun to shoot with her. When you get Carrie going, she still remembers all the lines from the old films, so she'll just launch into the opening of the first *Star Wars* where she's leaving the message in R2-D2. It's pretty incredible. It's all still right there.

John Boyega: Carrie was amazing to work with. She was like a mother towards everyone in terms of her attitude, in terms of her grace. She's so funny. You can talk to Carrie Fisher about anything, and she'll be so clued up on the subject. She's an amazing woman to talk to. So great to hang out and work with. She throws the best parties for the cast and crew. It was great to see the changes in Princess Leia. Princess Leia always had this strength and this focus, but was also a princess. As a *Star Wars* fan, I see the princess in her eyes but it's cloaked in this shell that reads warlord, warrior, savior, and intelligence. She has this golden maturity that you couldn't play if you hadn't been through thirty-five years of real growth.

Although Carrie Fisher sadly passed away on 27th December, 2016 her legacy continues to this day, with Leia appearing in numerous videogames and animated projects, with a talented array of actors taking on the mantle of the Princess.

13 /

12 / Rian Johnson directs Carrie Fisher as General Leia takes command in *Star Wars: The Last Jedi.*

13 / The voices of Leia (from left) Misty Lee, Julie Dolan, Shelby Young, Anna Graves, and Catherine Taber.

14 / Carrie Fisher as General Leia Organa in *Star Wars: The Force Awakens.*

Shelby Young (Leia, *Star Wars: Forces of Destiny*): Leia's voice was one I already knew well but had never tried to match. I only had one day to work on it, so I studied very hard, re-watching *A New Hope* and pausing and rewinding every Leia scene, and then reciting along with her dialogue.

Catherine Taber (*Star Wars: The Force Unleashed* series): I've always thought of Leia as a combination of Anakin and

LEIA ORGANA

Padmé. She can exhibit Padmé's grace and royal countenance, but she also has that super fiery and impetuous side that comes out, which she is less able to control than Padmé could. For better or for worse, I think Leia favors her father.

Julie Dolan (*Star Wars Rebels***):** One of my favorite lines was when Leia consoles Ezra after he learns that his parents were killed. He asks her why she fights when she doesn't have to because she is a princess. Leia replies, "I fight for those who cannot, and I think you might be the same way."

I love when Luke throws Leia his lightsaber in "Traps and Tribulations." Knowing that I voiced Leia's first canonical moment wielding a lightsaber is just insane for a fangirl like me. I also love "Bounty of Trouble," where Sabine tries to figure out how to properly address Leia when they first meet, stumbling between princess and senator, and Leia says it's just, "Leia," and follows up by saying, "I hope one day we can fight together." That line has always stuck with me. It really sums up her character."

Misty Lee (*Star Wars:* **Battlefront):** About halfway through the recording session I had to deliver the line, "Good luck—and may the Force be with you." I'd been doing fine until that moment, but as soon as that line appeared, I freaked. I started to hyperventilate. It's strange, but it kind of felt like Carrie was there, saying, "Just do it, kid. You've got this." I was immediately able to settle into doing the best I could. There were iconic things that Carrie did in those movies, like a head-tilt, that we really wanted to grab and honor.

I absolutely love Carrie's delivery of "Into the garbage chute, fly boy." She's so annoyed, and it's such a non-princessy thing to say. It's magic.

Catherine Taber remembers the same scene as being a defining moment for the character.

Catherine Taber: "Somebody has to save our skins!" is classic Leia. Calm under pressure, witty to the end, and no one's victim.

A Navajo translation of *A New Hope* **marked the first feature film ever to be dubbed into the language, with actress Clarissa Yazzie Garcia playing the role of Leia.**

15 / Leia (voiced by Misty Lee) takes arms during the *Star Wars: Battlefront II* version of the battle of Hoth released in 2017.

16 / Anna Graves provided Leia's voice in *Star Wars Rebels* (2014-2018).

17 / Shelby Young voiced Leia in four episodes of *Star Wars: Forces of Destiny* (2017-2018).

18 / Leia gets her hands on a lightsaber.

LEIA ORGANA

Clarissa Yazzie Garcia (Leia, Navajo translation): When Leia says, "Will somebody get this big walking carpet out of my way?" the translation for "big walking carpet" (*yaateel di'ili tsoh*) took me a few takes. It was something of a tongue twister to get the words out as quickly as I could, and still articulate each syllable. At the speed I was saying it, it sounded like I was saying "*dzi'izi tsoh*," which in English is "big bike!" I took a break and eventually got it right. That brief exchange with Vader encapsulated who she was, and right in that moment, I became Team Leia. Regardless of her circumstance, she was always strong and confident.

Julie Dolan: *Star Wars: The Empire Strikes Back*. *Empire* really helped me develop my Leia for *Rebels*. She was growing up. She was in charge of troops, learning to strategize, and discovering who she was in the Rebel Alliance. She becomes a tough soldier and falls in love!

Anna Graves (Leia, Disney Infinity 3.0): In *Star Wars: Return of the Jedi* (1983) Leia was in the thick of the action on Endor, fighting stormtroopers. I love the scene where she acknowledged what she'd felt all along, about being Luke's sister. And when she asked Han, "Hold me..." I just melt.

Shelby Young: Leia's story and growth throughout the Skywalker saga makes each movie she's in so special, because they take place at huge milestones throughout her life. I can't even compare *A New Hope* Leia to *The Force Awakens* Leia. She had been through so many life experiences that had ▶

LEIA ORGANA

19 /

> "I am Princess Leia. Princess Leia is me. It's like a Möbius strip."

19 / Fisher and her real-life daughter Billie Lourd pose on the *Star Wars: The Force Awakens* set with droid ally PZ-4CO.

20 / Carrie Fisher as General Leia in *Star Wars: The Last Jedi*.

made her grow and change, but at her core she knew who she was from the beginning.

I love that Carrie Fisher was never afraid to be 100-percent, authentically Carrie. She was outspoken about important subjects that so many other public figures tend to shy away from.

Carrie Fisher left a powerful and hugely influential legacy. Although much-missed, her performance as Leia continues to find and delight new audiences.

Carrie Fisher: I am Princess Leia. Princess Leia is me. It's like a Möbius strip. My life has informed who she is, and she's informed who I am and who I've had to be, based on experiences I've gone through and the courage that was required to go through some of that. So, a lot of her demeanor, her passion and her willingness to go on, I've found in me.

HAN SOLO & CHEWBACCA

HAN SOLO & CHEWBACCA

A smuggler who fights galactic oppression, Han Solo was played by both Harrison Ford and Alden Ehrenreich, always accompanied by the Wookiee Chewbacca, played by Peter Mayhew and Joonas Suotamo.

Despite numerous attempts to divide them, Han Solo and Chewbacca were inseperable since their first meeting on the planet Mimban to their fateful final mission on Starkiller Base. The scoundrel and the Wookiee, first played by Harrison Ford and Peter Mayhew, remain one of *Star Wars'* most beloved and enduring teams.

Kathleen Kennedy (President of Lucasfilm): [Han Solo] is very authentic. He's a scoundrel, he's a maverick, and there's a sense of mystery about him. Handsome, incredibly charismatic, and adorable—that's a pretty great combination for a *Star Wars* action hero.

Lawrence Kasdan (writer, *Star Wars: The Empire Strikes Back*, *Star Wars: Return of the Jedi*, *Star Wars: The Force Awakens*, *Solo: A Star Wars Story*): Han was always my favorite, right from the start. He's the most exciting guy in the saga for me. He's unpredictable. He's reckless. He's not particularly brilliant. He'll say things that he can't back up. He'll leap in when he should stay back. There's nothing more attractive to me than a screw-up who's actually got a good heart but hides it as best he can.

Mark Hamill (Luke Skywalker): I enjoy Harrison's character, Han Solo, the most. But then I think Luke also emulates Han, so there are parallels between the cast and the storyline.

Harrison Ford (Han Solo): [On first reading the script] I knew what *Star Wars* was going to kind of look like, but I didn't know how close they were going to come to it, or stylistically how they were going to approach it. I suspected what the style of the film was going to be, and the style of acting that would be called for. But I didn't know what the reality level was going to be. I thought of it as any old road movie.

I was one of these people who advances the story. This is the thematic function. I isolated the thematic function of Han Solo easily. It's not as easy to do it in other movies as it was in *A New Hope* and that's what I knew I had to do. It was how the character served the story.

It was real clear. to me. I don't know how to describe the picture of Han that I had in my mind, but I knew from the beginning what he was like. I just read it a couple of times and go in with what seems right and go from there. I'm not particularly aware of the elements of that decision. [It's intuitive to a certain extent], because otherwise there's no excuse for it at all.

Before we started filming in the *Millennium Falcon* cockpit, I asked George Lucas to let us get into it, so we could try it on for size. Finally, we did get a chance, Chewbacca [Peter Mayhew] and I, to walk into the cockpit and sit down. Of course, he was so tall, he couldn't get into the seat!

HAN SOLO & CHEWBACCA

1 / Harrison Ford and Peter Mayhew pose in character as Han Solo and Chewbacca in a publicity shot for *Star Wars: A New Hope*. (Previous spread)

2 / Ford shows off his blaster-slinging skills outside the Elstree soundstage.

3 / Han and Chewie take charge of the escape from the Death Star.

4 / Solo under threat from the hapless bounty hunter, Greedo.

5 / Chewbacca and Solo ready for action in the shadow of the *Millennium Falcon*.

▶ **Peter Mayhew (Chewbacca):** I started acting back in 1977. I had done a movie called *Sinbad and the Eye of the Tiger* (1977). I played the Minotaur. That was a wonderful opportunity. About six months later, I got a phone call that they were looking for a tall person for another movie. That led to an interview with George Lucas. George's office was enormous. I sat down on the sofa and when George walked in, I stood up. The interview was just about over at that point. George said that Chewie would do mime action. He can negotiate, but he doesn't make human noises. So, you have to watch what other people are saying and, consequently, you join it up with body action and this sort of thing. Then we went down to the creature shop and got a face mask done. The next day we went to a costume shop in London and got the suit made. Everything started to happen from that point on. It was a remarkable time in my life.

The first thing I filmed was the Docking Bay 94 scene at Elstree Studios in London. There was Harrison Ford and some extras, and an Irish actor named Declan Mullholland playing Jabba the Hutt in a scene that didn't make it into the initial release. There was sand all over the place, and it was a question of getting the shots as quickly as possible.

Lawrence Kasdan: I love [Han and Chewie's] relationship. I love all the qualities that are embodied by it. There's courage, there's teamwork, there's loyalty, and there's a slightly canted view of the world around them. Their relationship is reassuring, recognizable, and speaks to the best in each of them.

Jonathan Kasdan (Writer, *Solo: A Star Wars Story*): It's a great partnership. It's loaded with love. It's never cruel or hostile, there's a real intimacy.

Peter Mayhew: I'd say about 50% [of Chewie] was me and 50% was in the script. For example, in the *Millennium Falcon* cockpit, you've got four people in there. Chewie can't stand there looking like a piece of furniture. He has to react to everybody's attitude. And, he can't say what he wants to verbally, so he either has to use his mouth, or eyes or body language. So, that was 50-70%. I expected to be fired the first week! But, fortunately, George ▶

saw what I was trying to do and here we are many years down the road. It was fortunate that I was able to bring that to the character.

Working to bring George Lucas' vision of galactic civil war to life didn't faze Ford, despite the fact that the actor was more used to Earthbound roles.

Harrison Ford: [I had] no experience with science fiction, but I didn't find it any problem to imagine it. I was always keyed into the human context of the relationship. It wasn't as apparent to some audiences as it was to me that that was an important element. But that doesn't matter. It's a necessary foundation for fantasy to have some approach to it, some way of keying yourself into it, some accessible characters. But it's a very skillful conception, and I found it no trouble to deal with.

Ford was pleased to be able to make a contribution to the

formation of Solo's character over the duration of his involvement in the films.

Harrison Ford: We all had a certain amount of input once we got started. Over the course of making the *Star Wars* films, we worked with three different directors and each of them had a different style and different attitude towards the process. I would say that the relationship with those three different directors was different, but I always felt that there was a degree of collaboration that was comfortable for everybody involved.

Brian Daley (Writer, *The Han Solo Trilogy*, 1979-1980): Han is the only one who makes a moral decision in the course of the movie that changes him. Everyone else starts out bad and ends up bad, or starts out good and ends up good. He's the one who turns around in the middle of his departure and comes back.

HAN SOLO & CHEWBACCA

8 /

9 /

10 /

Harrison Ford: My part was more interesting in *The Empire Strikes Back*, so I enjoyed myself a lot more, even though it was a more difficult film to make.

Alan Harris (Double for Harrison Ford in carbonite): I played one of the Bespin guards who escorted the carbon-frozen Han Solo to *Slave I* and I provided the body for Han Solo in carbonite. Irvin Kershner said "Lie on the floor", they put two tubes up my nose and covered me in plaster! When it was finished they cut my face out and put Harrison's in.

In April 2011, Chewbacca made an appearance in the *Star Wars: The Clone Wars*, episode entitled "Wookiee Hunt."

Dave Filoni (Supervising Director, *Star Wars: The Clone Wars*): I had Peter Mayhew come up to Skywalker Ranch; I wanted the crew to meet him. I thought that you can't begin to understand how to make Chewbacca move, or who Chewbacca is, without meeting Peter Mayhew, knowing him a little bit, and seeing what he's like. So when you're working directly with George, and when he's looking at everything you do, that's the audience you have to please because he's the guy that created it all. When he's sitting in the theater and he's watching our Chewbacca and he says, "Well, I could tell when I looked at it that it was Chewbacca," that's really the validation that I think the crew hopes for.

Of the legacy characters that we featured in *Star Wars: The Clone Wars* I think that Chewbacca was the biggest deal. He is the character that has the most recognition, period. He's one of the classic characters. A character like Tarkin

6 / Harrison Ford discusses the scene "inside" the exogorth with director Irvin Kershner.

7 / Chewbacca and the droids in a publicity shot for *Star Wars: The Empire Strikes Back*.

8 / Chewie embarks on a mynock hunt.

9 / Ford flanked by rebel friends, including children cast as troops in order to give the cavernous Echo Base a sense of scale.

10 / Han, Leia, and Chewie face Darth Vader on Cloud City.

STAR WARS: THE GALAXY'S GREATEST HEROES | 45

HAN SOLO & CHEWBACCA

HAN SOLO & CHEWBACCA

© L.F.L. 1981
© L.F.L. 1981
HAN

12 /

11 / Han and Leia's romantic moment is interrupted. (Previous spread)

12 / Two sketches for Han's costume for *Star Wars: Return of the Jedi* by Nilo Rodis-Jamero

▶ requires you to be a lot more in the know in order to be aware of who he is. Chewbacca reaches a level close to Vader where families, kids, and people who don't really watch *Star Wars* regularly would know what you're talking about.

Keith Kellogg (Animation Director, *Star Wars: The Clone Wars*):
When we introduced Chewbacca, it was the first time the world had ever seen Chewbacca being performed by somebody other than Peter Mayhew. Peter was heavily involved in our recreation of the character and he gave us subtle ideas of how Chewbacca should behave. He is the only actor to have ever been Chewie and we tried to make sure we were true to his vision of the character. We made sure we incorporated the fact that he's not as aggressive as some of the other Wookiees, and he's a little more curious, and that he has the movie Chewbacca's little bow-leggedness. Hearing all that from Peter's perspective helped us to bring that character to life. There was also a technological advancement because we had moving fur for the first time. Chewbacca was an incredibly heavy character to animate; the animators struggled a bit at first, because of how dense he was, but we came up with ways we could help that.

Returning to the role of Han Solo in 2015's *The Force Awakens*, Ford was happy for the chance to impart his knowledge to actors starting out in their careers.

Harrison Ford: Daisy Ridley and John Boyega are both very

engaging personalities; both in their real lives and in their screen characters. They're both very inventive and spirited presences. Their characters are really interesting and the casting was brilliant, in both cases.

John Boyega (Finn): As he works on set, he has a great understanding of the artistic side of shooting a movie as well as the technical side of shooting a film. If anyone asks me what I have learned from working with Harrison Ford on *Star Wars*, I've learned that whatever film I go on to after this, shooting a film or a movie as an actor is a balance of the technical and the artistic. As an artist, you're portraying a role, being an actor, and performing. But the camera is the eye of the audience, so you have to also facilitate that. You have to facilitate the lighting, the positions and the visual effects. Harrison knows how to do all of that with great balance, but also have fun and make it a comfortable set. He hangs out with us after filming. I took him to South East London to a nice Nigerian restaurant. He spoke to me about all the things that he'd been through and all the things he'd seen over the years as an actor.

It was great to learn from an actor [like him]. He's a cool man.

Harrison Ford: J.J. Abrams was very thoughtful and very wise about human nature and the development of character and relationships. He brought a real sincerity and emotional understanding to relationships, which is something I was very pleased to see. He's an enormously skilled filmmaker and a very efficient director and producer. So it has been a real pleasure to work with him and all of the members of his team as this film has gone on.

Lupita Nyong'o (Maz Kanata): Working with Harrison has been precious. He knows this stuff. He's worked on this kind of big film many times before. He has shorthand with J.J. and the crew. To see him have such control, and yet be so playful. That's been so fascinating. On such a big set, with so many moving pieces, it's easy to get overwhelmed and not know what's going on. But Harrison always seems to know what's going on and zeroes in on that.

Harrison Ford: Larry Kasdan brought a lot of really fantastic opportunities to the character. He'd been working with J.J. Abrams on the script for a long time. He continued to be with us on the set and came up with some great stuff. I'm happy we had Larry on board.

Ford was also pleased to be reunited with some old colleagues.

Harrison Ford: I was very gratified when I first saw the script and thought there were some amazing ideas; interesting things to do. Then I was very excited for the opportunity to work with J.J. Abrams, whom I've known for a long time [Ford starred in *Regarding Henry* in 1991 which was written by J.J. Abrams].

I have a very long and fruitful relationship with Kathy Kennedy, so I was glad to be able to work with her again. I thought it was going to be fun. I knew that the film would be in good hands, but that wasn't the only attraction to the project for me.

We had discussions about development of Han and his relationship to other characters in the story. They were very interesting and encouraging conversations. Then there was some work done in respect of

13 / Han, Leia, and Chewie lead the rebel strike against the Imperial bunker on Endor.

HAN SOLO & CHEWBACCA

▶ the questions I had or input that I had with J.J. Abrams, and I was pleased with that. But I'm a "get on at the beginning and off at the end" kind of guy, so I don't really remember the street signs along the way.

With Ford returning as Han Solo, Chewbacca was played one final time by Peter Mayhew.

Peter Mayhew: It's extremely easy to get back into playing Chewbacca after a while. I don't know what happens, but once the costume is on, I get back into character very easily. It's happened on every shoot that Chewie's been involved with. I arrive on set, put the shoes on, and suddenly, Chewie is alive. I don't understand it, but it happens every time I do it. I wondered whether it would happen when I went down to Australia to shoot Episode III, and it did. The reaction from the crew was there, so I knew I was doing it right.

We knew we had to make a new costume because Chewie was younger. During the fittings we realized it didn't look right. The problem was that two shoulder pads were in the wrong position that gave him a bigger neck. We took those out and it altered the whole of Chewie's stance and persona. Chewie became Chewie again, rather than just another Wookiee.

Also performing as Chewbacca in *The Force Awakens* was Joonas Suotamo who would later take over the role full time from *The Last Jedi* onwards.

Joonas Suotamo (Chewbacca): I was aware of the casting for Chewbacca pretty early on, probably 2013, and after that I forgot about it because I didn't believe in my chances. I thought that they would find somebody else better suited. On top of that, I was busy at the time doing video work for my production company and I was finishing up selling insurance. I didn't see myself being

14 /

HAN SOLO & CHEWBACCA

to say, "Congratulations, you have the part."

Before going full time as Chewie, Suotamo took a masterclass on performing as Chewie from the man who knew the Wookiee best: Peter Mayhew.

Joonas Suotamo: It's an unusual situation to go into. I approached it as any team-work situation. I was a little nervous: Is he going to like me or is he going to think I'm this upstart trying to come in and steal his spotlight? But there were no issues like that. He was the coolest guy, and he gave me a lot of helpful tips. Not only Chewbacca-related, but going forward in my career. This is my first film and I took every chance I had to learn from him and the other actors. We only met a few days before shooting began, but it was effortless because we both had the same questions in mind. We were both interested in how the character was going to look.

I was always thinking about how to perform like Peter Mayhew, because that's what was important to me as a fan of the original trilogy. Peter is the greatest character. It's no surprise that Peter is so loved by the fans of *Star Wars*. He has a million wonderful stories to tell from the original trilogy and he shared many of those with me. He told me about the slight tucking down of the chin, which was one of the most important pieces of advice. I think that is the most visible trademark of Chewie. I don't know where it comes from. I guess it's because Peter is so tall and he didn't want to stumble over anything that was lying on the floor! Your visibility is somewhat limited when you have the mask on.

The sight of Han and Chewie in the *Millennium Falcon* at the coda of the first full trailer for *Star Wars: The Force Awakens* brought a lump to the throats and tears to the eyes of audiences around the world.

cast in *Star Wars* in the next six months! But, one day I received a call from the Basketball Association of Finland [Suotamo is a professional basketball player in his native Finland]. They had heard through their contacts that a big budget movie was looking to cast a seven-footer with blue eyes and they asked me if I wanted to send my photos in to this unnamed movie production. I just said, "Hell yeah!"

After visiting Pinewood Studios three or four times, meeting with J.J. Abrams, and doing all the costume fittings, they called me after some film tests we had done

14 / Harrison Ford as Han Solo in *Star Wars: The Force Awakens.*

15 / Ahsoka Tano and Chewbacca team up in *Star Wars: The Clone Wars.*

STAR WARS: THE GALAXY'S GREATEST HEROES | 51

HAN SOLO & CHEWBACCA

▶ **Lawrence Kasdan:** We were very pleased when we wrote that scene. There were so many moments in writing, and it took months and months of J.J. and I alone walking, talking, sitting, and writing. But we did it with a lot of walking around cities; Los Angeles, New York, Paris, and London. I've never written a movie that way. We were talking and recording, and then we'd go someplace and write it down. It was so much more fun than normal writing. We were sitting at a café in Paris, one of the famous cafés where Ernest Hemingway sat, writing *Star Wars*, with J.J.'s computer on the table. We wrote a lot of it walking around Santa Monica, ending up at the Palisades looking at the Pacific Ocean on a gorgeous day. We were doing all the difficult work of story construction, but we did it in incredibly pleasant circumstances. Once it was freezing cold, walking around Central Park. It was a heavenly experience.

Joonas Suotamo: The first day, entering the *Millennium Falcon* in the Chewie suit was surreal because Harrison was there, and everyone was excited. Walking up the ramp of the *Millennium Falcon*, arriving in the living room with the dejarik table. I just looked at it! I thought, *I don't want to bother anyone. I hope no one minds me being here.* Then I noticed people were looking at me and they just saw Chewbacca!

The people who made the suit did a fantastic job. Neil Scanlan said that nailing Chewbacca's look was one of the most difficult things he had to do for the movie.

Kathleen Kennedy: It was amazing for everybody. I was sitting by the monitors, near the door of the *Millennium Falcon*, and I turned around and there must have been 150 people from the crew who had all quietly gathered to get around the monitors and see that moment. It was very emotional. Everyone was feeling something slightly historic was going on. It really gave you chills. ▶

16 / Alden Ehrenreich and Joonas Suotamo at the helm of the *Millennium Falcon* in *Solo: A Star Wars Story*. (2018)

HAN SOLO & CHEWBACCA

HAN SOLO & CHEWBACCA

> "The genius of *Star Wars* has always been this science fiction fantasy context but underpinned by an emotionally recognizable human story that we all relate to to a degree."

2018's *Solo: A Star Wars Story* saw actor Alden Ehrenreich playing the younger Han as he embarked on a defining, early adventure for the hero.

Alden Ehrenreich (Han Solo): The relationship that Han has with Beckett (Woody Harrelson) is very important to him. Ultimately he learns how much he wants to be like this guy, and also kind of a reformed guy. In this film, he's still a freewheeling, outlaw pilot. You see a lot more of his style, a lot more of his ship, a lot more of his escapades. You see what he and his world were like before you met Lando in the original movies. Lando (Donald Glover) is a great foil for Han because they have a lot in common in terms of competitiveness, and the way they interact is really fun. It's complicated with them. That competitive streak only increases when they are up against each other. What you get to see over the course of the film is two alpha guys, who are each trying to be the fastest pilot. [Then there's] Qi'ra (Emilia Clarke), who is a dynamic character with a lot of mystery. You don't quite know what's going on with her, and neither does Han, and that's what keeps the tension going. Chewie and Han's relationship is really fun to watch because they act like an old married couple. But Chewie also has qualities that are like a dog: he's emotional and loyal—he really cares about Han.

Neal Scanlan (Creative Effects Supervisor): The team working on the film was so precious about being accurate and honoring the original Chewbacca suit, that the idea of throwing mud all over him and wetting him down seemed abusive. We got the hose out and literally doused Chewbacca down, and something magical happened—it made him immediately feral. He took on that sorrowful, bedraggled look, just like a domestic dog. It was interesting to see how quickly these animal qualities came out... and the whole premise is that he looks really animalistic: the beast of Mimban! He's been in prison for some time, he's covered in mud, and he appears first as a shape in the shadows. That's a terrifying experience for Han.

Ron Howard (Director, *Solo: A Star Wars Story*): There's a simple nobility and kind of clarity to Chewie. Not only is he an important co-pilot and a powerful figure to have in the trenches with you because of his terrorizing physical presence, but he does also have a conscience. And although Han learns from a lot of characters in this movie and those relationships help define who he's going to be a decade or so later, it is that quiet, barely articulated but fully demon-strated nobility that Han learns from Chewie. At the same time, Chewbacca can be terrified of things and have a horrible temper, and really needs to learn to chill. So, the fact that Han won't take him too seriously, or allow him to take himself too seriously, is probably a good thing for Chewie. He needs that.

Having played the character for nearly 40 years, Mayhew was able to offer a unique take on Chewbacca's enduring appeal.

Peter Mayhew: I think he's a big teddy bear and someone that could look after you if things started to go wrong. He's really loyal to certain people and yet he's quite capable of pulling his enemies' arms off and destroying stuff in a rage. Chewie's fans see him in lots of different ways. For some people he's a teddy bear, for others he's a hero, because he and Han would go in and just do things that only heroes would dare to do. A lot of fans love Chewbacca because he's so good in a fight! I don't even think Darth Vader would have messed with him.

Reflecting on his time as Han Solo, Harrison Ford recognizes the importance of the human element of the *Star Wars* saga.

Harrison Ford: The genius of *Star Wars* has always been this science fiction/fantasy context but underpinned by an emotionally recognizable human story that we all relate to by degree. We all recognize the power of these relationships, and the complications in people's lives, and it's made these films so important to pass on from generation to generation. You can call them family films, but they are iconic representations of what we know about the complications of our lives.

17 / Han and Rey head toward a fateful conflict at Starkiller Base.

OBI-WAN KENOBI

OBI-WAN KENOBI

A noble Jedi general and veteran of the Clone Wars, Obi-Wan Kenobi made his debut in *Star Wars: A New Hope* as played by Alec Guinness before Ewan McGregor and then James Arnold Taylor took on the mantle as the younger version of the character in the *Star Wars* prequel trilogy and *Star Wars: The Clone Wars* respectively.

A venerable Jedi Knight, Obi-Wan Kenobi was orginally played by Sir Alec Guinness, a theatrical knight himself. At the time of his casting, Guinness along with Peter Cushing was the most well-known actor in the film.

Alec Guinness (Obi-Wan Kenobi): The script came through the door and the minute I saw a sci-fi sticker on it. I thought, *Oh crumbs, this is not for me.* But when I started to read it, I had to turn the page. It had vigor and I finished it in one sitting.

Mark Hamill (Luke Skwalker): I was terrified to meet Sir Alec Guinness for the first time. I couldn't believe it. I went to a restaurant in London to meet him and thought, *If I open my mouth, I'm going to cry like a little girl.* I couldn't breathe. I kept calling him *Sir* Alec and he just finally got fed up with it. At one point he sort of tapped my face [to get my attention], twice lovingly, and the third time a little too hard for comfort. He stated, "I want to be known by my name, not my accolade." I replied, "Well, what do you want me to call you, Big Al?" That made him laugh. One of the things I learned about Sir Alec (see? I can't help myself) was that he had a great sense of humor. He loved people who were not pretentious and were comfortable with who they were. He was more proud of the Oscar nomination for his screenplay of *The Horse's Mouth* (1958) Than he was for winning [the Academy Award for Best Actor] for *The Bridge on the River Kwai* (1957). It was out of his realm; it was unexpected that he could be a screenwriter as well. I kept asking him about his career but he would say, "No, no. I want to hear about *your* career." I thought, *You want to hear about a dog food commercial, a soap opera, and a TV series that got canceled after four episodes?*

Guinness was impressed by George Lucas' professionalism.

Alec Guinness: Before we started filming, [George Lucas] made a gesture that was much more a part of the theater than the film business. He brought the costumes for the film across to London himself to see if I liked them and he attended all the fittings. That is exceedingly rare.

Guinness was always supportive of George Lucas during the shoot.

Alec Guinness: [During filming] I remember somebody criticized George Lucas because of his lack of display and announced that the film was going to be very dull. I took that person aside and said, "Mark my words, this film is going to have some distinction." George Lucas is like all the best directors. He had very little to say during the actual filming. He simply sensed when you were uncomfortable, walked across and dropped a brief word in your ear. Good actors don't like to be told how to act.

The day before *Star Wars* opened in America, George Lucas phoned and said, "Do you know, I think we have got quite a success. The press quite like it."

Mark Hamill: I was so lucky to work with someone I admired for

OBI-WAN KENOBI

2 /

The fight scenes were not the only challenge that McGregor faced, with George Lucas's notoriously complicated *Star Wars* dialogue proving a unique hurdle for the actor.

Ewan McGregor: The dialogue is quite difficult to say as an actor. There are a lot of scenes with heavy dialogue where we have to put our heads together to make them work. It's not enough that the right words are said and the information to put across. It all has to make sense and the conversations have to be ones that the characters would actually have. I think that is what we have done well—we made the scenes work. A lot of the dialogue is expositional and that is always difficult for an actor because it involves saying something to an actor who knows this stuff already. Hayden and I would be discussing something that our characters would both know so the conversation is really only for the audiences benefit.

A lot of my vocal performance was done later in the ADR room because there's so much noise and wind machines going on when making the film. I'm not an actor that enjoys massive amounts of ADR, which is where you revoice the scene. In this case it has been quite handy because some of the action stuff made it very difficult to sound like Alec Guinness.

1 / Ewan McGregor as Obi-Wan Kenobi in a publicity shot for *Star Wars: Revenge of the Sith* (2005). (Previous spread)

2 / Behind the scenes as Sir Alec Guinness and David Prowse battle as Obi-Wan and Darth Vader in *Star Wars: A New Hope* (1977).

3 / Guinness and Mark Hamill on the Dagobah set prior to the shimmering Force Spirit effect being added in postproduction for *Star Wars: Return of the Jedi* (1983).

4 / Alec Guinness delivers a pivotal speech in Ben Kenobi's home on Tatooine.

so long. He was so gracious with his time. He stayed in contact, writing to me with beautiful calligraphy in old-fashioned ink. I would see him in London, and we'd go out to dinner. He was one of the greatest actors ever.

For the *Star Wars* prequel trilogy (1999-2005), George Lucas cast a young Scottish actor to play the young Obi-Wan. Perth-born actor Ewan McGregor was of a generation that had grown up watching the *Star Wars* saga as a boy.

Ewan McGregor (Obi-Wan Kenobi): They said, "Do I want to be in *Star Wars*? I said, "Too right!" My challenge was to be a young Alec Guinness. He was amazing. It all goes back to him really. I just think about how he played his scenes in Episode IV. Really, the choices he made for the character are still his today.

I watched the original *Star Wars* over and over again. I loved it as a kid. It was funny to be paid for it. I'd say to my wife, "I've got to go and watch *Star Wars* again! Sorry. I just haven't quite got it…"

Unlike his predecessor, McGregor underwent rigorous training and rehearsal in order to perform the action-packed lightsaber battles. Despite being well-practiced, the fight sequences did not always go to plan.

Ewan McGregor: My lightsaber flew out of my hands. No one tells you they have got batteries in them! They burn your hands! I tossed my saber in the air and it ended up hitting a technician on the head!

3 /

OBI-WAN KENOBI

OBI-WAN KENOBI

5 /

Much like his predecessor, McGregor enjoyed George Lucas' approach to directing.

Ewan McGregor: I like George Lucas because there's no messing about. There were no 100 takes of me walking through a door. He knew what he wanted and when he got it, we moved on.

Star Wars: Attack of the Clones (2002) marked a first for the actor as he reprised his role as Obi-Wan Kenobi who found himself at the heart of galactic mystery.

Ewan McGregor: Doing *Attack of the Clones* was interesting, because I'd never had to go back to play a character again. It was three years between the two episodes. It was a bit easier because I was more used to the technical demands. In other films you rehearse, crack the scene and shoot it. In *Star Wars*, that's not the case. It's a very different process with an enormous amount of blue-screen work. It's very difficult—you play scenes with people who aren't there.

Appearing in the *Star Wars* films brought out a certain playfulness in the actor, who, at that point had been better known for dramas such as *Trainspotting* (1996).

Ewan McGregor: I love being in *Star Wars*, for my kids and for other kids. I see it through their eyes. During a press junket, I managed to convince a Dutch journalist that we were shooting Episode II entirely in outer space!

The completion of *Star Wars: Revenge of the Sith* (2005) saw McGregor take a break from playing Kenobi for nearly 20 years. The character flourished in animated form as James Arnold Taylor gave voice to the Jedi as he fought in the Clone Wars.

James Arnold Taylor (Obi-Wan Kenobi, *Star Wars: The Clone Wars*): Originally, I was hired for the 2003 *Star Wars: Clone Wars*

5 / Obi-Wan Kenobi faces his destiny in *Star Wars: A New Hope* (1977).

OBI-WAN KENOBI

6 /

6 /

6 / Ewan McGregor as the younger Obi-Wan Kenobi in Star Wars: The Phantom Menace (1999).

7 / A master and his apprentice, Obi-Wan and Anakin in Star Wars: Revenge of the Sith (2005).

8 / Obi-Wan aboard The Invisible Hand.

9 / McGregor films Obi-Wan's high speed battle with General Grievous.

micro-series to be an exact voice match for Ewan McGregor. We basically have the same sound, the same range. So I thought that rather than trying to sound like him, since I know I already do kind of sound like him, I'm just going to do what he did: try to sound like Alec Guinness. So I started thinking of how he would talk, and I tried to young it up. I thought, *OK, so if I was casually speaking as a young Obi-Wan, I might sound like this*. I didn't concentrate so much on sounding like Ewan McGregor as much as I concentrated on sounding like Obi-Wan Kenobi, the character we all know. That seemed to work. You can get hung up on a voice match where you try too hard to sound like the person and it becomes a caricature. It becomes more the nightclub comic's impersonation. You want to relax in the voice. You really have to understand how that person would act, and you have to be able to act that way. I always have to envision how he would deliver the line. It's more than an impersonator would do, because you have to understand the character and be able to say anything in that voice.

Arnold Taylor's performance impressed series creators George Lucas and Dave Filoni, as the Obi-Wan was developed further.

James Arnold Taylor: Dave Filoni and George Lucas said, "You have the freedom now to take this and make it your own thing." Dave's vision for Obi-Wan in *The Clone Wars* is very specific. He's trying to show Anakin the right way, but he's also the calm in the storm all the time. I'm always the straight guy. Most of the time, I'm pulling the reins back on Anakin and Ahsoka, so I'm like the older brother that's trying to be the parent. Nothing really gets to him. But at the same time, I know people may think sometimes he's a little too reserved, so I'm trying to give him some excitement. Every once in a while, I would torture myself and read the message boards to see what people like, and some people do think he's got to lighten up. But I just think, *Give him time*.

The ffocus on the relationship between Anakin and Ahsoka meant that it took time for Obi-Wan Kenobi to be explored.

James Arnold Taylor: Obi-Wan is such an iconic figure, but you don't know anything about his personal life. We had so many episodes to do, so it took time for the writers to explore those areas. *How does he act when he's gotten up on the wrong side of the bed and he's having a bad day? What's his day-to-day relationship with Anakin?* It's been fun to work with everybody and create those parts of his life and his characteristics. I try to put a little of what will become the reserved old Jedi living alone in this deserted part of a desert planet, into the young one who was in the world and so much a part of everything in his earlier life.

The steadfast Jedi enjoys a strange relationship with Sith acolyte Asajj Ventress during *The Clone Wars*.

Dave Filoni (Supervising Director, *Star Wars: The Clone Wars*): I've always wanted Obi-Wan Kenobi

and Asajj Ventress to have this bizarre flirtatious relationship, even though she's kind of the bad apple and he's the good guy. With the changes to Ventress' character, it makes you wonder what would happen if they did meet again and what kind of situation would draw them together.

That's one of the exciting things about the dynamic changes to Ventress' character over the course of the show. I'm not saying she's a good guy—*hardly* ! She learned a big lesson on the trail with her master, Count Dooku which left her with a lot of room to grow in many different directions. So it was interesting to see the characters we know so well, like Obi-Wan, reacting to those changes.

James Arnold Taylor: Oh yeah, there's a lot of playfulness between those characters. I mean, they really get to flirt! Fans often ask me: "So what's the deal between Obi-Wan and Ventress?" [Adopts Obi-Wan voice] "*Well, I can't possibly say….*"

Also, Nika Futterman [who plays Ventress] is such a fantastic actress. In fact, the very first scene we recorded was the one you see in *The Clone Wars* film, where she and I are having our battle. She brings me up to a different level as an actor.

James Arnold Taylor has his own views as to the enduring appeal of Obi-Wan Kenobi.

James Arnold Taylor: It's his accent! And his charm! Actually, I think that the biggest reason is the prequels. The prequels kind of turned Obi-Wan into a leading man, even though the story is about Anakin and Darth Vader and the Skywalkers. I think that he had a new grace with Ewan McGregor, and now *The Clone Wars* has taken the character even further. ▶

9 /

Obi-Wan constantly attempts to keep everybody on track, but he also tries to be realistic. You saw that in "The Citadel" episode in Season Three where they're losing clones left, right and center. I remember when we were in the studio voicing that stuff, Dave [Filoni] kept telling me that Obi-Wan is the one who says we must move forward and we have to keep going. I had to strike a balance when recording those lines to show he has sympathy and heart for the clones, but at the same time he knows the mission. I think that sums up the character: he's a strength when other characters don't necessarily know what to do, and he's a voice of reason.

10 /

9 / McGregor, producer Rick McCallum, George Lucas and Ahmed Best on set for *Star Wars: Attack of the Clones* (2002).

10 / Anakin and Obi-Wan battle over the lava on Mustafar.

11 / Hayden Christensen and Ewan McGregor in *Star Wars: Attack of the Clones* (2002).

12 / Erik Tiemans art showing Obi-Wan astride a varactyl in *Star Wars: Revenge of the Sith* (2005). (Next spread)

The process of making the show changed quite a bit over the course of seven seasons.

James Arnold Taylor: It's changed a bit over the last seasons. Some of that comes from working on such a tight schedule, but it's also due to the top secret nature of it. Generally speaking you'd get scripts 24 hours in advance, but eventually we got them when we arrived at the recording session.

But we did get the chance to go through everything before the session starts. Dave sat down with us all as a cast and went through the story, and then talked to every person there, whether it was a guest star or whether it was Matt [Lanter], Ashley [Eckstein] or myself who are there every week. He took his time with each person and gave us pictures or descriptions of what's happening, and provided background on the episodes either side of the one we're recording. It really helped. That approach also added to our ability to change things. Dave might have said, "Oh that doesn't really feel like Obi-Wan. What if he said this instead?" Or I might have said, "This is a great line as it's written but when I say it, it doesn't come out right." There was a freedom for us all to act as we might on camera.

The process of recording was intense, though. As voice actors, we really had to think on our toes. We ran through a scene three to eight times on average, and try to make it different each time.

As the series progressed, Arnold Taylor found himself impressed by the high standard of the storytelling.

James Arnold Taylor: When he did the "Mortis" episode, my reaction was, "Wow, this is something we haven't ventured into before!" I really admire Christian Taylor's writing and storylines. The writers take it from a viewpoint that it's live-action. And with the technology they have now, the animators can do that–they're making live action in a virtual world.

OBI-WAN KENOBI

OBI WAN KENOBI

▶ A close bond between Padmé and Obi-Wan forms over the course of *The Clone Wars* run. Arnold Taylor felt that there was potentially more to their relationship.

James Arnold Taylor: Catherine [Taber, who plays Padmé] and I are such good friends and we always joked around with Dave saying, "Come on, man, we've got to see a [romantic] episode!" Because in Episodes I and II Obi-Wan thinks she's a politician like Palpatine, and doesn't buy what she says. But then somewhere down the line there's a connection and a bond that's made between them. In the show we explored what happened and why they're closer by Episode III.

Though the Jedi Master's iconic dry wit often featured, Arnold Taylor would like to have brought more humor to the show.

James Arnold Taylor: Ewan [McGregor] did have some great moments, especially in the elevator scene in Episode III; Obi-Wan was having fun! You could see that

OBI-WAN KENOBI

have aimed for your neck," and "I like your new legs. They make you look taller." Because I know James so well, I can picture James saying this. Screening the episode with an audience, you realize you need that so the audience thinks, "Oh, he's going to be okay." Obi-Wan takes that punishment and moves on. I think it says a lot about his character. He is very tough, despite his more elegant way of speaking, which doesn't mean he's not a physically tough and mentally tough Jedi. He carries that burden for years in the desert alone. We are watching the formative years of Obi-Wan. He was in a lot of scrapes and he did take a lot of punches, so that old man on Tatooine is almost hesitant to get back in the fray. "I'm getting too old for this sort of thing," he says, because he knows what it's like out in the big galaxy to be fighting for everyone's freedom. These are dark times. I think Qui-Gon summed it up: Being a Jedi is a hard life.

Surprisingly, Obi-Wan found himself in a romantic entanglement with a Mandalorian duchess.

James Arnold Taylor: I had some fun banter with Anna Graves, who plays the Duchess Satine Kryze. Anna is such a talented actress. She and I had done promo work in the past, and for us to have a good old battle of words was great!

I love the comedy in their relationship. Like that bit in the second part of the "Duchess of Mandalore," when Obi-Wan is hanging upside down and about to be crushed, and he says: "I'm a little tired up here!" But there's also a love between those characters, too. I think that's the main thing—we joke with the ones that we love. Obi-Wan has a heart for all of the characters, and I tried to keep that in mind when I'm doing it, so it doesn't come across as too mean or snarky.

playful nature in his relationship with Anakin—you could see they're like brothers, not father and son. We got some of those moments in The Clone Wars now and again, too. Several times each season Obi-Wan had a quip that just cuts through and you're like, "Oh *behave* Obi-Wan!" So it's definitely there, but it would be fun to see a bit more.

I play Plo Koon as well as Obi-Wan, and they're very serious parts. I'm so honored to play these two Jedi because they hold such weight in the storyline, but it would be fun to have a character who could go a bit more crazy every once in a while, too!

Dave Filoni: Obi-Wan is a really fun character, especially with James Arnold Taylor playing him. He does such a brilliant job. Obi-Wan, in a way, is one of the characters who will let you know that when things are really bad, it'll be okay. And things got really bad for him. He has to shoulder the burden all the time in *Star Wars*. Not just when he's being captured by slavers or transformed into a bounty hunter, or has a nemesis from the past come back. He's shouldering the burden of knowing he didn't finish the job. That he left Anakin alive, and because he did that, how many untold terrible things have happened in the galaxy? Is that because he's compassionate, and because Anakin's his friend?

In the Darth Maul arc, originally, Kenobi was totally getting brutalized in that ship's hold by the two brothers. The director, Brian Kalin O'Connell, had him being thrown against these metal boxes, and dragged across the floor. I thought, *Whoa, this is intense*. Imagine that scene with no little snappy comebacks from Obi-Wan. So I sat in editorial and added a little dialogue here and there, like Obi-Wan saying, "When I cut you in half, I should

13 / Rehearsing the climactic fight in *Star Wars: Revenge of the Sith* (2005) with co-star Hayden Christensen.

14 / Obi-Wan Kenobi in the Jedi Temple, shortly before discovering his apprentice, Anakin Skywalker, has turned to the dark side in *Revenge of the Sith*.

15 / Some of the team behind *Star Wars: The Clone Wars*, including James Arnold Taylor (Obi-Wan), Ashley Eckstein (Ahsoka Tano), Dave Filoni (supervising director), Cary Silver (producer) and Dee Bradley Baker (the clones).

16 / Obi-Wan battles his nemesis, Sith acolyte Asajj Ventress!

17/ The long-form storytelling of *The Clone Wars* enabled Obi-Wan to take center stage in many episodes.

18 / Obi-Wan clashes lightsabers with General Grievous. (Next spread)

▶ As the show progressed, Arnold Taylor discovered there were a few surprises in store although Obi-Wan's ultimate future was not one of them.

James Arnold Taylor: Obi-Wan is one of those parts where I'd think, *How do I play this?* Because the story takes place inbetween Episodes II and III; I know what happens in III, but I couldn't let that affect my acting of him here. I think that Obi-Wan feels—and this is the way I played it—that [the attraction to the dark side] is always going to be a part of Anakin and any other Jedi. But Obi-Wan knows the strength of Anakin and thinks he'll overcome it.

I don't think Obi-Wan expected anything that happened in Episodes III to V. I think he was so trusting in Anakin and the Force; he had hope and faith. I really don't think he expected the dark side to be so heavy and actually take away Anakin from him. And, of course, that's a pain that we see in Episode III.

We always think of Yoda as his teacher and instructor, but really the father to him was Qui-Gon. When we had the surprise of Qui-Gon appearing in the "Mortis" trilogy, I was like, "Oh this is so awesome!" And what a great honor to have a scene with Liam Neeson!

When we did that scene I actually, very subtly, youthed my voice up a little. I went back to *The Phantom Menace*, watched that a lot, and gave the voice a slightly lighter and softer tone. Because Obi-Wan reverts back to when he was younger—I thought he would be very off-guard and revert back to when he was with his master.

**Ironically, the actor didn't actually get to work with Liam Neeson, a situation not untypical on animated productions.
James Arnold** ▶

STAR WARS: THE GALAXY'S GREATEST HEROES

OBI-WAN KENOBI

▶ **Taylor:** Liam was in New York when we did it, and he recorded his part there. It's funny: that is such a heavy part of voice-acting. I mean I've been able to work with just about everybody in showbiz today, but usually the scenes are recorded completely separately so I never get to meet them. Take Patrick Stewart and Samuel L. Jackson—I've been in five or six projects with each of them, and yet we've never met. Even though most of our scenes feature the two of us having conversations together! One of these days it would be fun to meet them–but alas, that's the work of a voice actor!

A veteran of seven seasons of *The Clone Wars*, Arnold Taylor is proud of the legacy of the show.

James Arnold Taylor: *Star Wars* is essentially about a dramatic series of events: they're fun and exciting, but there's also a lot of intensity to them. Even if you go back to *Star Wars: The Empire Strikes Back* (1980) when Han Solo's put into carbonite —that's dramatic and compelling. As a kid I was like, "He's gone! He's dead! They've killed Han!"

I think with the way filmmaking has progressed, we were able to push things so much further now with *The Clone Wars*. The drama in it feels real, and it also goes back to Dave Filoni and George Lucas' vision, which tells us that life is sometimes filled with challenges but if you keep on the right path, you will always prevail. They made *The Clone Wars* into exciting, compelling TV that you want to come back to.

The Clone Wars has taken it to a whole new level. It's like those sci-fi adventure shows that I love, such as *Lost*, *Battlestar Galactica*, and *Heroes*, which have that level of drama, realism and characters you care about. Well, the makers of *The Clone Wars* created that in 22 minutes every Friday night! I think that not only goes back to the writing, but also the artistry of it all. ✦

AHSOKA TANO

AHSOKA TANO

From a Padawan learner to a Jedi to an exile from the Jedi Order, Ahsoka Tano's emotional journey gave Ashley Eckstein a opportunity to create a unique character in the *Star Wars* saga.

Making her *Star Wars* debut in the 2008 *Star Wars: The Clone Wars* movie, Ahsoka Tano soon became a much-loved character in the *Star Wars* mythology. When we first meet her, she is an effervescent youngster placed under the mentorship of Anakin Skywalker. Ashley Eckstein's performance as the character would take the young Togruta in a multitude of surprising directions., not least when she brandished two lightsabers!

Ashley Eckstein (Ahsoka Tano): Two lightsabers are always better than one! I thought that was awesome that she got a second lightsaber. One of them is shorter, almost like a lightsaber dagger, which I thought was really cool. She definitely toughend up. She spent so much time with Anakin, Obi-Wan, and Plo Koon that she began taking on their fighting skills, especially Anakin's. Ahsoka has no fear, no fear at all. She just goes right at it. Sometimes Anakin is so spontaneous that he doesn't think about the Jedi way of doing things. Obi-Wan is more by the book. Ahsoka is definitely a combination of them both.
I wouldn't say Anakin is a bad influence, but he's not necessarily *the best* influence for promoting the Jedi way. Anakin does things his own way, so Ahsoka has definitely become more like Anakin. At times she acts in ways that would be against what they would teach at the Jedi Temple. But thinking outside the box like Anakin and Ahsoka do is sometimes the best way to accomplish what you want. You have to take the good with the bad.

The third season of *Star Wars: The Clone Wars* featured a trilogy of episodes set in the mysterious world of Mortis.

Ashley Eckstein: The scripts of the three Mortis episodes really blew my mind. I couldn't believe that they were allowing us to tackle that storyline. There are some heavy questions about Anakin and who he is. It really affects the movies and ties them into our series. I think that's what was so nice about our show—as we went along, we helped explain things that happen in the movies and answer people's questions about why things are the way they are.

When we first started, some fans complained because our show would be part of *Star Wars* canon, but now I think they welcome the fact that they're getting some answers they always wanted. I had to approach them differently because Ahsoka goes through many personality transformations during this story. She grows up, and she goes through some extremely tough times. Just having to explore those different personalities, but still keeping them true to Ahsoka, was quite difficult for me. There was one scene I wasn't quite hitting on the first try. Usually when we record ▶

AHSOKA TANO

an episode we only do three takes of every line, and then we move on. It's rare to do more than three takes of something, but this one particular scene we were doing over and over again. I was getting really frustrated that I couldn't nail it. I was so blessed to have James Arnold Taylor [Obi-Wan] in the studio with me. He came over and said, "Okay Ashley, calm down, you can do this. Try it this way," which was completely different than how I was doing it. It worked and that's the take they ended up using. It was like going to school every time I went into a recording session. I'm constantly learning from the cast. The animation in that particular scene just blew my mind. The animators continued to raise the bar, but they really went to town for the Mortis episodes. There's some stunning shots that we truly haven't seen before.

As an actress you always look for challenging opportunities and roles. As the cast all became more and more familiar with our characters, it could have become routine because playing your character becomes second nature. We'd been working on the show for five years, so you automatically know how your character would say certain lines. To have opportunities that are challenging and [that] give you the chance to stretch your talents is definitely something that I always looked forward to. Putting Ahsoka into different situations, whether she seems evil, or whether she grows up, or exploring where she is heading is something that can be very rewarding to perform.

When *Star Wars: The Clone Wars* drew to a close after six seasons, it seemed like the end of the road for Ahsoka, until Eckstein was

1 / Ahsoka Tano (Previous spread)

2 / Ahsoka and Captain Rex have a bond that crosses two seperate shows.

3 / Another battle droid gets taken down by Ahsoka!

4 / Anakin and Obi-Wan meet Anakin's new Padawan for the first time

AHSOKA TANO

tipped off that she was to return in the new animated series, *Star Wars Rebels*.

Ashley Eckstein: It was a hard secret to keep. I kept the secret for about a year, and it was so tough because I didn't lie to the fans, but I couldn't tell the truth so what do you really say? When friends would ask me over and over again, "Is Ahsoka going to be in *Rebels*? Are we going to see Ahsoka again?" I would just have to say, "Well, you know, she's still alive. It's kind of too soon to tell. You know, they're still writing *Rebels*. Who knows? Maybe we'll see her one day."

Once Fulcrum came into the storyline, it was harder to be vague. The fans—who are so fantastic—pitched up Fulcrum's voice and said, "Okay, that sounds like Ashley and the way that she

AHSOKA TANO

5 /

speaks!" I pretty much went into hiding after that because I didn't know what to say. I kind of avoided interviews, all podcasts, really all social media about the subject, until after the finale aired because I didn't know what to say about it, and I didn't want to lie to people.

For Eckstein, there was a feeling of unfinished business as she returned to play an older, wiser Ahsoka.

Ashley Eckstein: I'm a huge fan of the characters in *Star Wars* and so, as a fan, I became so invested in them. We spent six seasons on *The Clone Wars* getting to know these characters so deeply—we really did. They're animated characters, but we became emotionally attached to them. I can't say enough about Captain Rex and what he means, but also Hondo Ohnaka is a personal favorite of mine. So for *The Clone Wars* to end like it did, kind of on a cliffhanger and not knowing where these characters ended up, it meant so much for them to come back in *Star Wars Rebels* because we needed more from these characters. We need more of their storylines, we need to know where they went and what they've been doing, and what happened to them.

The show reunited Ahsoka with her former ally, Captain Rex.

Ashley Eckstein: They have a bond like family. They really spent so much time side-by-side fighting in *The Clone Wars*. I think Ahsoka has such a special bond with Rex because he was kind of like a mentor in a way, along with Anakin—even though she said in the show, "So, if you are a captain and I'm a Jedi, then technically I outrank you, right?" Rex quickly put her in her place and said, "Well, experience outranks everything," and I think she respected him from day one for that and admired that she had to earn his respect. I think along with Anakin and the rest of the gang, it's like an older brother and a family member. So they have a really, really tight bond and we don't know what happened between them after she walks away from the Clone Wars, but we do know that they're both still alive, and we did get to find out more about what they've been doing since.

6 /

5 / Ahsoka confronts Obi-Wan and Anakin in combat after being infected with the dark side of the Force.

6 / Going into battle with R2-D2 at her side.

7 / The actress behind the voice of Ahsoka, Ashley Eckstein.

8 / Ahsoka and Jedi younglings. (Next spread)

AHSOKA TANO

9 /

▶ *Star Wars Rebels* also features the return of Darth Vader, a character with a unique and disturbing relationship to Ahsoka.

Ashley Eckstein: Darth Vader is a newer presence to the rebels. He is the most powerful, and as powerful as I think Ahsoka is—and of course I am biased—it's still Darth Vader [laughs]. Dave Filoni told me that if Ahsoka and Darth Vader were to eventually confront each other, that it probably wouldn't be a good thing for Ahsoka. Dave said on the *Rebels* panel at *Star Wars* Celebration that, obviously, it's a natural progression for her story. I feared for her because of that advice Dave Filoni once gave me!

Eckstein saw parallels between Kanan and Ezra's relationship and Ahsoka and Anakin's.

Ashley Eckstein: I think Kanan and Ezra have a bond that is like Ahsoka and Anakin's in that it is unbreakable, and that can't be replaced by Ahsoka. I think how I would almost describe it is how Ahsoka was with Obi-Wan. Ahsoka and Anakin were really close, but Obi-Wan was this wise adviser that Ahsoka almost cowered to a little bit, because there was so much respect—like he was the master to the master, if that makes sense. There was like an extra level of respect there; she was always on her best behavior around Obi-Wan. She always watched her manners and Ps and Qs, and she wasn't too snippy with Obi-Wan. I almost think Ahsoka will be viewed by Ezra with a sense of reverence of, "She is this master to the master," essentially. Ahsoka's

10 /

9 / Ahsoka and the crew aboard the *Ghost*.

10 / A vision of a potential future for Ahsoka.

11 / An older and wiser Ahsoka as she appears in *Star Wars Rebels*.

12 / Ahsoka meets Chopper

AHSOKA TANO

not that, but I'm just saying, Ezra has more of a friendly relationship with Kanan with the banter and the wisecracks.

Being a veteran of *Star Wars: The Clone Wars* Eckstein was able to advise the new cast as to what they might expect when they first appeared in front of the fans at *Star Wars* Celebration.

Ashley Eckstein: I remember the first Celebration for the whole cast of *Star Wars Rebels*. I was giving them advice backstage like, "Okay, here's what's going to happen, and here's what we are going to do and here is what to expect!" They all had several questions. Right before they walked out on stage for the panel, they were like, "Oh my gosh, we can't believe all the fans out there," and they were nervous. It's definitely like life imitates art. I felt like Ahsoka— I was able to provide advice because this was my fourth time appearing at Celebration.

Having played the character since 2008, Eckstein still feels an affinty to Ahsoka.

Ashley Eckstein: There are so many lessons that I've learned from Ahsoka. Sometimes it feels silly to say that this animated character has taught us so much, but she really has. I look up to her. I often think, *What would Ahsoka do?* I feel like she has such a good heart and such a good moral compass that she'll always choose what's right, and I often keep that in mind. But I think Ahsoka came back with a sense of confidence in *Star Wars Rebels*. It's almost like when we go to school for so many years and then when we graduate, we're out in the real world. It's like Ahsoka is now out in the real world, and we now see her in her job and she is very confident in it. I think that's what we can take from her right now in *Rebels*: Just be confident in what you're doing and go forward with the story.

AHSOKA TANO

▶ Following Ahsoka's storyarc in *Star Wars Rebels*, which saw her confronting her former master Anakin Skywalker, now reborn as the Sith Lord Darth Vader, there was another surprise in store as it was announced that *Star Wars: The Clone Wars* was to return for one final season.

Ashley Eckstein: I first heard about it from Dee Bradley Baker. I was at Disney World riding rides with my husband, and I got this text message. I knew that Dee was wine tasting with the *Star Wars Rebels* cast and that Dave Filoni was there, so when he sent me the text message and he said, "Clone Wars, 12 episodes coming back," I didn't believe it. I was like, "That is top secret news." I forget exactly how the text chain unfolded, but Dee was like, "No, no, for real. This is happening." Of course, I was excited because if Dee is telling me that it's for real, then I want to believe him because he is like a brother to me. I heard from my agent next, and I still didn't believe it. I said, "Wait a minute, I haven't heard it from Dave. This can't be real." So, I called Dave and he said, "Hey, what's going on?" I said, "Do you have something to tell me?" Dave felt really bad. He said that wasn't how he wanted me to find out, but that it was true, and I was so excited. I didn't fully believe it until I heard it from Dave Filoni.

When *The Clone Wars* was canceled, it was so sad. We didn't get the proper goodbye. We didn't get that final recording session or that happy wrap party. So, I took *The Clone Wars*, locked it in a place in my heart, and I threw away the key. I was so hurt and didn't want to allow anyone to hurt us again. When I found out that it was happening, I was in absolute disbelief. Obviously Dave Filoni was crucial to it, but one person that is the unsung hero, that is not getting the credit that she deserves, is Carrie Beck (vice president of animation and live-action development at Lucasfilm Ltd). I'm forever grateful to the fans for not giving up on the show, I'm forever grateful to Carrie Beck for believing that it could come back, I'm forever grateful to Dave Filoni for getting the gang back together, and I'm forever grateful to Disney+ for giving it a home. Though I'm usually an extremely very positive person, I was not so positive about *The Clone Wars*. I never thought it would ever come back. It's kind of ironic that the last fortune cookie caption for the last episode in which Ahsoka had appeared was, "Never give up hope, no matter how dark things seem." The fans never gave up hope. They always had hope that *The Clone Wars* would be saved, and here we are. They took that very last fortune cookie to heart.

In order to make the show, Eckstein and the cast were briefed by Dave Filoni, who shared his knowlege of the saga and how it would link to *The Clone Wars*.

Ashley Eckstein: Before we started, Dave [Filoni] would come in and he would give us a 20 to 30-minute breakdown of each

13 / Ahsoka pilots the *Ghost*.

14 / Ahsoka and Ezra Bridger discuss their next move.

15 / *Star Wars Rebels* featured a dramatic confrontation as Darth Vader confronts Anakin Skywalker's former apprentice.

AHSOKA TANO

16 /

> "We're all professionals, but there was so much joy. So much laughter, so many jokes, so much acting up, so much silliness!"

16 / A surprise inclusion in *Star Wars Rebels*, Ahsoka's journey would continue far beyond her animated adventures.

17 / Ahsoka during the Clone Wars era.

episode. That's how I learned *Star Wars*. I've been a lifelong *Star Wars* fan, I grew up loving *Star Wars*, but I didn't know it like I do now. Dave would always tie the breakdowns to other parts of the saga. I learned so much. Those moments were like lost episodes. He would tell us what our character was going through, what emotional space we were in, what head space we should be in, what our agenda for that episode was for our characters. What were they trying to say? What were they trying to achieve? What were they going through? It was truly a deep dive into each episode.

We're all professionals, but there was so much joy. So much laughter, so many jokes, so much acting up, so much silliness! But also, so many emotions. The episode records got very deep at times. They got very sad, very emotional. When we were recording *The Clone Wars* before, we knew that we had so many episodes ahead of us. There was never that thought of, "This is the last one." We never had the countdown, but with these last 12, we did have that countdown. Every single time we walked into the studio, it was one step closer to the end. There was a bit of sadness every single time. Dave really had to keep us in check because we brought an essence of sadness and deepness to these episodes

Eckstein briefly reprised her performance as Ahsoka during the climax of *Star Wars: The Rise of Skywalker* (2019) as the Jedi reach out to Rey.

Ashley Eckstein: I found out I was doing it a couple days before I went into the studio. I walked into the theater at Bad Robot, and there was Matthew Wood [supervising sound editor] and J.J. Abrams, the director. J.J. shook my hand and introduced himself, and immediately thanked me for being in the movie. I couldn't believe it.

J.J. said, "Being a voice actor, obviously you're not on set, you're not physically acting a scene out, so what do you visualize when you read your lines?" I can't say that it's necessarily something I visualize, it's actually a feeling that I have. I know when my voice is in the right spot. I can feel it. My own voice, as in just Ashley Eckstein, sometimes it's too high pitched. I get too excited, I go too high, so I have to tone it down a bit. There's a feeling I get when I know that I'm in the right vocal range for Ahsoka, and I also feel it when I know that I'm not.

YODA

A Jedi Master like no other, Yoda's debut in Star Wars: The Empire Strikes Back *took the world by storm as audiences met—and fell in love with—an icon of good as much as Darth Vader is an icon of evil.*

Yoda was an audacious gambit that could have brought audiences' suspension of disbelief crashing down had it not worked. Thankfully the combined efforts of actor Frank Oz and makeup maestro Stuart Freeborn ensured the Jedi Master was all too real.

Stuart Freeborn (Makeup and special creature designer): When I first saw him, I loved Yoda. I thought he was going to be the greatest creature ever. The drawings by Ralph McQuarrie varied quite a bit. Some I liked, and some I wasn't too keen on. One or two showed Yoda with a suggestion of a little twinkle in his eye that said to me that this little guy was looking at me and sizing me up and already had me pegged! I felt that I had to capture that look and make Yoda look wise and a likable sort with a slight smile, but still sarcastic where he can twsit up his mouth and just play games with you, that switch back to being the nice old fellow that he really is.

With the clock ticking down to the start of filming, Freeborn drew some inspiration for the look of the character from a source that was very close to home.

Stuart Freeborn: Things were getting very tight with production due to start very soon. George Lucas came to my workshop one morning and asked if I could have a go at creating a design for this little fellow who was secretly a powerful and wise warrior. The catch was that he needed to see it that afternoon as he was flying back to the States! I had a sculpture of my own head that I had been working on and thought about modifying that. I added the ridges to the head as George had described the character as very wise and I thought they might indicate thought. Also, anything can happen on another planet. On Earth, if you have scales you don't have hair but Yoda has both. I thought I could make him a bit different as he is an alien after all. I thought that many years ago his species came from the sea, as did man originally, and they retained some of the scales. You would never see an earth creature with both. I didn't see why Yoda couldn't have both—he had to be different after all.

The trouble was, he didn't look alien enough. I was wondering what I could do to make him look alien, but without losing his character and charm, and then I had a flash of inspiration and added the ears.

I always figured that I had a burlesque comic, jovial look. I'm a little bit funny looking but not bad. I wanted Yoda to have that funny looking quality but at the same time, I wanted him to look wise. I don't think I'm particularly wise looking so I down to sculpt Yoda's face with a picture of Albert Einstein and a mirror an drew inspiration between the two. I'd study my face and Albert's face—everybody knows he was a genius. I put as much of him as I could into Yoda. My ears aren't as long as his but they do stick out a bit!

When George came back that afternoon, I had covered the sculpt under a large wet rag. He asked to see the piece and I took the rag off and covered my eyes, convinced that he would hate it! I'd never modeled anything so quick. I thought, *It's going to be a load of rubbish.*

He looked at it very carefully and, as he did with Chewbacca, said "Yes! That's it" and that's how Yoda was born.

A longtime friend, who assisted George Lucas and Gary Kurtz in the marketing of *Star Wars***, Edward Summer was privy to the genesis of Yoda.**

Edward Summer (marketing consultant): Gary Kurtz lived on a road called Elusive Drive in Los Angeles, and he called me up in a panic one day asking for a ride to the airport. This was after *Star Wars* and before filming had

YODA

2/

started on *The Empire Strikes Back*. He said, "I have to go to a meeting about the new *Star Wars* movie first. If I take you, you have to swear that you won't say anything about it."

We drove to Jim Henson's house. They had a meeting out in the backyard with Jim Henson, Frank Oz, and David Lazer, who was the producer on *The Muppet Show* and a lot of the movies. The meeting was about how to realize Yoda for *The Empire Strikes Back*. I really knew very little about *Empire* and I wasn't even familiar with who or what Yoda was. He was supposed to be a squirrel-like character—very small, fast-moving, and fast-talking. Gary wanted to have a scene where Yoda is jumping in and out of Luke's backpack, and needed Jim and Frank to create some sort of puppet to do this. But there were issues with using a Muppet. How do you hide the puppeteer? The second problem is that the traditional Muppet is a rod puppet; it has two stiff black wires that go up to the hands. In

3/

YODA

the context of *The Muppet Show*, the audience just accepts that; it's perfectly acceptable for Kermit's hands to be manipulated that way.

In *Empire*, the goal was for Yoda to be completely real. It would be one thing for Yoda to pop out of a backpack, but it was a whole other thing for him to jump from the ground into the backpack or to ride around on Luke's shoulders as he ran through the swamp. They also wanted Yoda to be able to walk and to have real legs. There was a lengthy discussion about how Yoda could be a large puppet operated through the floor, but that would involve having slots or some kind of opening in the floor of the stage. They were concerned that if they used dry ice to create fog it would fall through the slit in the stage and you'd be able to see it, like a waterfall of fog. After a while, Jim joked, "Gee, if you decided to merchandise this character after the film comes out, you could have something called a toy-Yoda!"

Some time later, I was visiting with Stuart Freeborn at Elstree Studios. I'd met him when I was editing the first *Superman: The Movie* magazine in 1978. I'd spent almost a whole day with him talking about all the flying props and special effects for *Superman*. This day, he and Wendy Midener (who later married Brian Froud) showed me the rubber head for Yoda and a beautiful Wookiee headpiece. They had several of everything, in case there was a failure on the set, so they could immediately pick up a second prop and go on with the shooting. Frank Oz walked in; it was the first time he had ever picked up the Yoda puppet and he tried it out. The way the "black rod" problem had been solved was by putting Yoda's hand on his staff so that Frank could do hand gestures the way he would with any other Muppet. The first thing they filmed was the scene inside Yoda's house, which had been built in the middle of one large sound stage, and was elevated above the floor. Mark Hamill could barely get in there, because it was a tiny little space, but the floor was open because the Muppeteers worked with the puppets straight over their heads while looking into a monitor. I remember Frank clearing his throat and trying different ways of speaking.

Performing as Yoda was a grueling though eventually rewarding experience for Frank Oz.

Frank Oz (Yoda): Yoda is very hard work. It's really five days of rehearsal for two days of shooting, because every single move, every

4 /

1 / Yoda, the Jedi Master, as seen in *Star Wars: Revenge of the Sith* (2005). (Previous spread)

2 / Luke undergoes training with Yoda.

3 / Yoda and R2-D2 tussle over Luke's flashlight.

4 / Ralph McQuarrie's art depicting Yoda and Luke in the Jedi Master's home on Dagobah.

YODA

YODA

5 /

blink has to be worked out. You have to really fine-tune it before you get on the set, and it's physically hard to do. But Yoda became an old friend. It was nice to revisit him and to dig a little deeper into his character, because it's more acting than performing. Muppets I perform more With Yoda I act more, in the sense that I trust the script and the character more and I'm not thinking about pleasing the audience. It's also nice being on a juggernaut like *Star Wars*. It's fun bringing the character to life and working with George. I have several places where I really feel at home in my life and I'm fortunate that this is one of the many homes that I have, and it's nice to go back to. *The Empire Strikes Back* was two weeks of shooting and my scenes for *Return of the Jedi* took two days to film.

Despite his efforts, Oz is keen to point out the real reason that he believes Yoda is such a success.

Frank Oz: On thing that people don't understand and really should is that so much of the reason that Yoda was successful is because Mark Hamill believed and responded to him. If Mark didn't respond to him so well then the audience wouldn't have.

Ever the perfectionist, Stuart Freeborn was always working to improve the Yoda puppet between the two films.

Stuart Freeborn: We always had two Yodas on call, just in case. If we had problems with one, we would just rush him off and have his stand in take over. to keep the cameras going to as much as we could. In the movies, everything is a prototype. You can never feel that you have the final stage in whatever you do. I suppose everytime we make anything we try to improve it and make it run a little easier than before. The last Yoda we made for *Return of the Jedi* ran a lot better.

5 / The Jedi training scenes from *The Empire Strikes Back*. Frank Oz credits Mark Hamill's interaction with Yoda as the key ingredient in bringing the character to life.

6 / Obi-Wan and Yoda watch as Luke leaves Dagobah in this production art by Ralph McQuarrie. (Next spread)

7 /

▶ Following the release of the original trilogy, George Lucas embraced new technologies, but held back on digitizing Yoda.

Frank Oz: I thought George should make Yoda a digital character. I thought it would save me a lot of trouble—my arm wouldn't hurt so much. When he was preparing the Star Wars prequels, George said he wanted me to operate the puppet Yoda on *Star Wars: The Phantom Menace*. As long as the character is true and pure, that's the most important thing. As long as he doesn't look like an effect it's a case of whatever works for the audience.

Much-loved for his work as Miss Piggy, Fozzie Bear and countless others on *The Muppet Show* (1976-1981), Oz is well aware of the special connection between the two franchises.

Frank Oz: They both had a vitality and purity and joy and dreaming. there was genius behind both of them. George worked with Jim on *Labyrinth* (1986) and they were united in creativity.

Oz was pleased to reprise Yoda sixteen years later for *The Phantom Menace*.

Frank Oz: It was fun working with Samuel L. Jackson, Liam Neeson, Jake Lloyd, and Ewan McGregor. But I was so involved in trying to do everything right

8 /

that I just talked to then between takes. We didn't spend a lot of time together but I admire their work a lot. I was hooked from the second page of the script for The Phantom Menace. I thought the script was really excepional. And George's work was so good in the edit that I knew he was going to make it even better.

I never thought about whether I would play Yoda again. But when you do a character that's strong in your heart, it carries through underground for many years, it can come up again. I didn't have to think of Yoda all of the time to be aware of him. When the time came again to play Yoda, it was like riding a bike. If an actor knows a character, they are always there.

The voice is only 10 percent of the performance. Making the performance work on the shooting day is the hard part of playing the character.

Yoda was realized as a digital character in *Star Wars: Attack of the Clones* (2002) and *Star Wars: Revenge of the Sith* (2005), and later replaced the puppet used in *Star Wars: The Phantom Menace*. He would later make a surprise appearance in *Star Wars: The Last Jedi* (2017).

Neal Scanlan (Creature and special make-up effects creative supervisor): Our philosophy right from the start was that Yoda was too iconic to change, but how could we update the puppet? We set about uncovering every bit of information we could about what Stuart Freeborn had done with the original, and why he'd done it, so that we could emulate that and make an absolute replica.

7 / Yoda commands the clone troopers as they rescue the Jedi.

8/ Yoda confronts Count Dooku.

9 / Promotional art for the National Public Radio production of *The Empire Strikes Back* illustrated by Ralph McQuarrie.

YODA

We were able to resolve some of its minor problems to make a puppet that was more user-friendly, but from the exterior ours was completely faithful to the original. We rehearsed with Frank Oz, but I felt something wasn't right about the puppet and it was driving me insane. You can build these phenomenal mechanisms with flexible skin, but unless the two come together in the perfect way, you won't get the best out of either of them. I said to Frank, "This isn't how the puppet is going to look on the day," and I did something you're never supposed to do in this industry—I put Yoda in my bag and took him home with me. I sat with him for an entire Sunday and walked through the same steps Stuart must have done, unpicking the skin here and re-gluing it there, not quite where it was meant to be—and suddenly Yoda came back to life. We had done what Stuart had done, which was basically glued the skin down until it looked like Yoda. Shooting that sequence with Frank Oz has to be one of my career highs, no doubt about it.

Although he eventually passed away in 2013, Stuart Freeborn followed his creations career over the years as Yoda gained fame beyond the *Star Wars* films.

Stuart Freeborn: It's astonishing to see that they created an animated Yoda, and I was surprised and delighted when he made it onto a stamp! Not bad for a little fellow!

The 2008 *Star Wars: The Clone Wars* movie and it's subsequent seven season run saw the voice of Yoda being provided by acclaimed voice actor and dedicated *Star Wars* fan Tom Kane.

Tom Kane (Yoda, *Star Wars: The Clone Wars*): The Yoda thing just kind of happened. I was in the studio playing another character for s LucasArts videogame. I'm a Star Wars nerd, so I would sit looking through my script and I would try to do my best Grand Moff Tarkin or Boba Fett voice. I was goofing around one day and I saw some Yoda lines, so of course I was trying to do some of my very best Yoda voice. As I was doing it, the producer looked up and said, "Can you do that again?" What I didn't know was that Frank Oz was very busy at that point because he had become a very successful film director. So, they played my Yoda performance for George Lucas and he gave his approval and I suddenly found myself performing as Yoda for videogames and that led to toys and commercials. That led to three seasons of the Star Wars: Clone Wars micro-series that ran from 2003 to 2005. When the time came for *Star Wars: The Clone Wars*, somebody said "We're going to use Tom."

10 / Yoda, as he appears in *Star Wars: The Clone Wars*.

11 / The character was voiced by Tom Kane, who narrates the start of each episode.

12 / A fan favorite who is also a pop-culture icon, Yoda won a whole new audience thanks the show.

13 / Yoda and the clones. (Next spread)

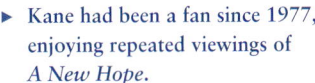
YODA

14 /

► **Kane had been a fan since 1977, enjoying repeated viewings of *A New Hope*.**

Tom Kane: It was the last day of school in the ninth grade when the first *Star Wars* movie came out in 1977. The world changed for me the day I first saw it. Within 10 seconds, when that Star Destroyer came overhead, I just sat there with my mouth hanging open going, "Whoa!" I think I saw the movie 12 times. I took my mom, and then I took my grandmother. She said "Oh honey, I don't watch those types of movies," and I said, "Grandma, you will love this." and she did. When the other movies came out over the years, we went to see them.

Kane was revertial about taking the iconic role.

Tom Kane: I look at it, not just as a cool gig, which it is, but as a honor to be entrusted with something so iconic with a voice that is well known throughout the world. James Arnold Taylor who is the voice of Obi-Wan Kenobi is also the current voice of Fred Flintstone, and something we talk about is how honored we are to be gatekeeping there characters and their voices. It's not something we created, so even though it might not be ours, it's on loan. I may be Yoda for another couple of years, it's up to George but for as long as it lasts, I just tried to do it the justice that it warrented and hoped that everyone would be happy with it.

Tom Kane: I would have loved to have done Darth Vader, but he is so hard to do. There is a quality to James Earl Jones voice that is just impossible to duplicate. My Vader is alright for a line or two but it's not oing to fly for any length of time. Yoda has to be number one though. Anytime it's a character who is important in the films , that adds a bit of extra weight for me, emotionally., because as soon as I hear the words and hear the voice—even if it's me doing it—brings back the joy of seeing the movies. ☻

14 / Yoda's final moments as he becomes one with the Force.

LANDO CALRISSIAN

Suave, debonair, and charismatic, Billy Dee Williams portrayal of Lando Calrissian in the original trilogy created a cape-swirling icon before Donald Glover played the character as a younger man.

Already a respected actor prior to his casting in *Star Wars: The Empire Strikes Back*, Billy Dee Williams was only too eager to joining the *Star Wars* cast as the morally ambiguous Lando Calrissian.

Billy Dee Williams (Lando Calrissian): During the 1970s there were all these new, young, extraordinarily talented filmmakers emerging, such as Steven Spielberg, Francis Ford Coppola, and Martin Scorsese. I was really looking forward to working with George Lucas. As an actor, you are always excited to be doing interesting things, and I got really lucky to have the opportunity. I mean, he's one of film's great innovators.

Before I was cast as Lando I was under contract to [legendary Motown Music founder] Berry Gordy, and it was through him that I worked for George Lucas.

The Empire Strikes Back had great production value, a strong look, and a powerful script. I think Irvin Kershner, our director had a lot to do with it.

I don't remember any real discussions about how to interpret Lando. They let me go. They trusted my interpretation. There were other concerns they had—all the technological stuff, the blue screen. So it seemed to me they left it to the actors to develop the characters. All the actors had personalities that really worked for what they were trying to convey. Lando's unparalleled charm is his greatest asset, of course! That was one of the things that I thought was very important to that character.

Williams was pleased to wear the distinctive cape that would become synonymous with the character's sense of style.

Billy Dee Williams: When I got that cape, I really tried to use it as much as I could. That was a key factor as far as finding the character was concerned. It reminded me of all those wonderful swashbuckling movies I used to see when I was a kid, with Errol Flynn. That was exciting for me. The cape was something to work with and something interesting to play around with and find the character through. When I wore the cape for the first time, I made it very much a part of Lando's persona. I mean, Lando has style. There's no doubt about it!

I think Lando was like a Steve Wynn. When he had Cloud City, he was running something that was comparable to Las Vegas, and he was very wealthy and running the whole show, so he was quite a businessman. But he was a great gambler. Oh, and the ladies were there. There were an awful lot of ladies!

Much of Lando's charming persona was derived from Williams' himself.

Billy Dee Williams: Well there's an awful lot of Billy Dee in Lando. I think I'm a pretty charming guy. I don't take myself seriously, and I think that's a good thing. I've always admired men who were subtly cool. I loved Duke Ellington. But he was also very entertaining at the same time. I've always wanted to play

LANDO CALRISSIAN

2 /

1 / Billy Dee Williams in a publicity shot for *Star Wars: The Empire Strikes Back* (1980) (Previous spread)

2 / Williams, Carrie Fisher, and Mark Hamill film aboard *Millennium Falcon*.

3 / Lando and Nien Nunb lead the attack against the Death Star II.

3 / Lando checks on the recently carbon-frozen Han Solo.

4 / Lando helps Leia in a desperate attempt to save Han.

5 / Williams joins the cast for *The Empire Strikes Back*.

Ellington. I came very close to playing him a few times. It should have happened. I think I'm the only one who could really pull it off, because the guy was such an interesting individual, and I understand that kind of charm. I don't know if there are any other guys around today who really understand it.

From gambler to Baron Administrator to general, Lando has adopted many roles over the course of the saga.

Billy Dee Williams: That's movie magic. It's very interesting—he becomes a general, and why he became a general was never explained. I mean, there was no army to really speak of.

Williams is a popular guest at *Star Wars* conventions.

Billy Dee Williams: I have a lot of fun. I absolutely and totally enjoy them. I remember when William Shatner said, "Don't these people have a life?" But what I've discovered is that a lot of them do have a life! A lot of them are just big fans, who are very bright people. I find it very interesting. I have never in my life wanted to be that kind of a fan for anything, but thank goodness those people do exist.

I don't have the same career I had then. But my career still somehow exists as a result of those experiences. We actors love to be patted on the head, told how wonderful we are—we live our lives for that. It's great when I do a Q&A and the place is packed. It makes me feel good.

You know, people sometimes ask if it bothers me to always be recognized as Lando, but I

LANDO CALRISSIAN

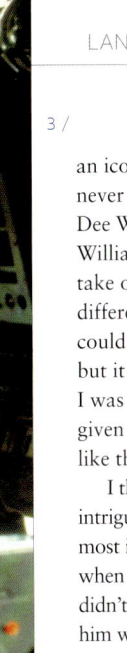

an iconic character, but I was never going to play him like Billy Dee Williams. I'm not Billy Dee Williams and he isn't me. My take on him is probably way different. I guess in a way it could be considered daunting, but it never felt that way to me. I was just really excited to be given the chance to play somebody like that.

I think that Lando is a really intriguing character. He was the most intriguing character to me when I was a kid, because you didn't really know if you could trust him when you met him. Sometimes he's a good guy and sometimes he's a bad guy. He's only beholden to himself. People like Lando because it's always nice to meet people in life who have flair and style. I think it's a lot of work to put that much style into your everyday life. You have to really care about things, and it shows that you care about perception in life in a different way. I think there's something about Lando that's really graceful and cool.

I would say that he's a very particular person, very prim and ▶

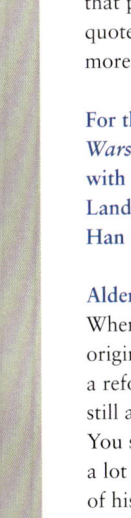

succeeded in creating a character that people remember and people quote from. You can't ask for more than that.

For the 2018 movie, *Solo: A Star Wars Story*, Lando was recast, with Donald Glover playing Lando as he first encountered Han Solo.

Alden Ehrenreich (Han Solo): When you meet Lando in the original movies, he's kind of a reformed guy. In *Solo*, he's still a freewheeling, outlaw pilot. You see a lot more of his style, a lot more of his ship, a lot more of his capes. You see what he and his world were like before you met Lando in the original movies.

Donald Glover (Lando Calrissian): I wasn't really nervous about taking on the Lando role. He is

LANDO CALRISSIAN

proper. He's very smooth; he's very self-assured, and he's the type of person who could be the life of the party if he sees it as being advantageous to him.

Like Williams before him, Glover was much in favour of Lando's wardrobe, with his penchant for capes expanded upon in the prequel.

Donald Glover: Lando definitely has the best clothes! It was great to wear all those costumes. It was really fun to actually be him, to focus on the character and make something unique. I had a blast being Lando. From the hair to the capes to the boots and the whole style, it felt very comfortable.

The film elaborated on the relationship between Lando and his friend and rival, Han Solo.

Donald Glover: They don't trust each other, but they have a common goal. They have friends in common, and they have people they care about. They are acquaintances who care about each other, but at the end of the day they are also in competition with one another, which I think is complex, but also very real. Good movies need a release valve, so I think comedy is important. There should be something that feels light when there's darkness in the story. I thought it had a lot of heart and presented a view of why people do things. I felt like it hit the sweet spot of being something that everybody could understand, while also being true to the world—not necessarily our world, but very specific to human nature, which I really liked.

The object of the two men's rivalry is the *Millennium Falcon*, Lando's ship that eventually changes hands.

Donald Glover: The *Millennium Falcon* is Lando's really cool bachelor pad, not to mention a great party ship. It has a large living room with an area for drinks and food, as well as a stereo system and gaming station. The bedroom has a huge closet filled with what seems like a million capes. If I were traveling throughout the galaxy, this is definitely the ship I'd want to be in. I can imagine landing, letting the ramp down, and having people just hang out inside.

Billy Dee Williams returned as Lando for the final chapter in the *Star Wars* saga, pleased to be back to save the day one last time.

Billy Dee Williams: Our director, J.J. Abrams, is so imaginative, and so much fun to work with. Making *The Rise of Skywalker* has been one of the high points of my career.

6 /

6 / Donald Glover as Lando Calrissian.

7 / Billy Dee Williams returns as Lando in *Star Wars: The Rise of Skywalker*.

8 / Production art by Ralph McQuarrie showing Lando and the rebels trying to rescue Han Solo (Next spread).

LANDO CALRISSIAN

LANDO CALRISSIAN

PADMÉ AMIDALA

PADMÉ AMIDALA

Natalie Portman's portrayal of a young queen, whose devotion to her people is matched only by her love for a certain young Jedi, laid the groundwork for tragedy.

A teenager when she first appeared as Padmé, Natalie Portman's distinctive look comprising of a multitude of outrageous hairstyles, bold make-up, and lavish outfits was one rivaled only by Darth Maul as one of the most iconic images associated with *Star Wars: The Phantom Menace*. On receiving the role, the actress had to get up to speed up on her *Star Wars* knowledge.

Natalie Portman (Padmé Amidala): I watched all of the *Star Wars* movies after I had got the job—I had seen parts and obviously it's part of the culture so I knew about Princess Leia's buns, and lightsabers. I knew key words but didn't really know the gist of it. I was really excited because they were so cool. They showed a shift in filmmking that was really new, and George Lucas was the first director to go in that direction of those really big films using technology to make images of things that you can't do on set and to make it look real. I thought it was amazing—now it's still impressive because if the nature of the story but when it initially co,me out it was the first of its kind. George has an amazing sense of what he is doing before he does it. A good director has a vision of what they want before they film it. George is amazing like that.

The actress soon discovered what a big deal *Star Wars* was to many people, including some closer to home.

Natalie Portman: Some people really make *Star Wars* a lifestyle. I know people whose lives are *Star Wars*. Everything about their life is connected somehow. I never really thought about it that much until I was a part of it, but people really make it a huge part of their lives. I had a friend who was in the same grade as me who told me that he bought the *Star Wars* Trivial Pursuit. He was saying that he was reading the questions and and one of the questions was something like "Which star of Episode I had their Sweet Sixteen on June 9th, 1997?" And he found my Sweet Sixteen invitation and was freaking out! I was like, "OK, you've known me since I was 13, you shouldn't be quite so impressed!"

Playing a character so young, yet in such a powerful position of authority brought with it numerous challenges.

Natalie Portman: George told me his biggest struggle with Amidala was to make it believeable that a 14-year-old would be Queen. No one could doubt she could be a Queen, so we worked a lot on voice and posture, all the movement and facial expressions to make it very stern. Even though it's already more acceptable because its a par of the *Star Wars* universe, I think it was a little less ▶

2 /

1 / Natalie Portman as Padmé Amidala in *Star Wars: Attack of the Clones*. (Previous spread)

2 / Queen Amidala, ruler of the Naboo.

3 / Taking arms against the Trade Federation on Naboo.

4 / The decoy Amidala confers with the real queen.

questioned because of the stuff we worked on.

Carrie Fisher's portrayal of Leia, Padmé's daughter, in the original trilogy helped Portman create her performance.

Natalie Portman : It came into play how strong and smart a character Carrie Fisher portrayed, because I think that a lot of that is passed on from parent to child. George wrote Amidala as a strong, smart character, but it helped to know that I had this great woman before me who had portrayed her character as a fiery woman.

Appearing in the saga has given Portman an insight as to why the saga has touched so many lives.

Natalie Portman: I think *Star Wars* appeals to people because it has very basic themes that are central to everybodies lives. *What is good? What is evil? How do they interact and change us and shape usas human beings?* The big *Star Wars* themes are these forces of good and evil—the Force and the dark side, and that they sometimes come out of balance.

Portman was pleased that *Attack of the Clones* would see Padmé go in a slightly different direction.

Natalie Portman: I was very excited that she wasn't going to be a queen anymore, because it allowed the character to be more like a real person, as opposed to this regal façade of a person. It starts out that her relationship with Anakin is one of mentor. She's known him only as a little boy prior to this episode; so when they re-encounter each other, she

3 /

114 | STAR WARS: THE GALAXY'S GREATEST HEROES

PADMÉ AMIDALA

treats him like a little kid. George worked with me to make me seem older than Anakin, to make it believable that she would boss him around and look at him as a little boy—at least for the first half of the film, until it becomes more of a romance.

In this film, Anakin was played by Hayden Christensen.

Natalie Portman: I was really impressed by Hayden. He was very confident. I was scared that he would be intimidated because it's a *Star Wars* film and that would make him nervous but he wasn't.

I didn't do much perparation besides reading the script and going over my scenes. I usually think that knowing the story and understanding the what's happening in a scene is enough preparation. I'm not super-serious about my work I don't want to take it too seriously because I think that part of the fun of *Star Wars* is that it's got issues within it, but it's a light film.

I wouldn't say that good versus evil was the main theme of *Attack of the Clones*. That film was more of a love story than anything else. But there is a foreshadowing of Anakin's dark side—it's a major factor actually.

***Attack of the Clones* utilized new techology to aid production.**

Natalie Portman: It was pretty exciting to be working with digital video. Having scenes run on monitors as they're being shot saves a lot of time on the set. It was great for hair, make-up, and wardrobe because they can see the exact colors or for the director of

PADMÉ AMIDALA

▶ photography because he can see the exact lighting. For actors, I don't think it changes that much because I never watch myself after I do a scene. It makes me too self-concious, so I don't really deal with those monitors too often. It's great to be on a film like *Star Wars* because you realize how little a part of everything you are as an actor! Usually on films you are the center of attention but being in *Star Wars* puts you in your place because realize that it still takes two years after you finish shooting until the film is done. You learn to respect the entire crew because you realize how big a part every person plays. There were so many people working on the film, it was very exciting to see the finished product because it's like seeing a movie for the first time. You see all the sets and characters and it's like a completely different film from the one you made!

Portman's experiences on *The Phantom Menace* prepared her for the special effects intensive sequel, *Attack of the Clones*.

Natalie Portman: Having been through the experience of making *The Phantom Menace* and then seeing it, helped. I didn't understand what anything was going to look like or what the characters would look like or why it was important to keep a certain eyeline. It didn't even cross my mind. Bu now I've seen the images and how amazing they are, and how real the characters are, I felt like I could really interact with them.

There was a lot of bluescreen on *Attack of the Clones*. Pretty much every set had a bluescreen element to it, even if it's just a window or something. The key is simple—it's imagination. That's why bluescreen acting is maybe the purest form of acting. It's like being a little kid in a cardboard box pretending it's a spaceship. That's the point you have to get to—pure imagination. If I were a really amazing actor (laughs) it ▶

5 / Natalie Portman as Padmé.

6 / Palpatine and the queen observe the Senate as Captain Panaka looks on.

7 / Queen Amidala in her formal attire.

8 / Anakin and Padmé's forbidden romance blossoms in the fields of Naboo. (Next spread)

9 /

9 / Ewan McGregor joins Portman on set as George Lucas looks on.

10 / A behind-the-scenes shot as Padmé narrowly escapes death.

11 / Padmé Amidala makes a return to the Lars' homestead on Tatooine in *Attack of the Clones*.

would be incredible to work with greenscreen because I could totally rely on myself to create the word around me. The lazy actor in me really appreciates having a beautiful set to act in.

We had a speeder we were working on on one of the first days and it looked so cool. It seemed more like a ride than a set. It had all these buttons and gadgets and we got so excited and wanted to touch everything but none of them were real. You'd go to press a button and it was just a little square pasted on that didn't do anything!

With the story taking a darker twist as Anakin suffers a dramatic fall from grace, the plot offered Portman a chance to play challenging scenes alongside Christensen and Ewan McGregor.

Natalie Portman: The scenes with Anakin were the most challenging because they were all very similar. I wanted to make sure that it didn't seem like there was just one issue that we were dealing with—I wanted to make it seem like we had a real relationship. Hayden is really great to work with. He was really impressive. What was most impressive to me was his "stuntability" I watched them film one of the fights between him and Ewan McGregor and he seemed as good as the stunt guys. In the first two films, the scenes I had with Ewan usually involved other people, and they didn'r involve anything other than a formal encounter where I played a queen or a senator and he played a Jedi paying his respects. This time around he would do things before filming that would help me or push me, which was really helpfuland very generous of him to do so. He was great.

While the threat of Padmé's death duting childbirth is the catalyst for Anakin's turn to the dark side, Portman plays down her involvement.

Natalie Portman: I don't think you can say that someone elses decisions or actions are caused by a particular person but I think everyone's environment shapes them. Everyone who ever came into Anakin's world had some effect on him that led him to where he ended up, especially Padmé, being such a central part of his life from a very young age, probably influenced him a little bit.

The mood of Padmé's final scene, as she finally expires after giving birth on Polis Massa, was lighted by Ewan McGregor.

Natalie Portman: There were animatronic babies [that were eventually replaced by real babies]. Ewan is the Frank Oz of the new millennium because of his baby puppeteer tricks. He did the scenes while talking and being very serious, yet all the while moving the baby in his hands. It was pretty amazing.

10 /

11 /

In 2008, the *Star Wars: The Clone Wars* movie spearheaded a new animated series, with Padmé voiced by actress Catherine Taber.

Catherine Taber (Padmé Amidala): We tried to use what was already there [in the films], which I think is important when you're doing anything like *Star Wars*. Dave [Filoni, *The Clone Wars* supervising director] was really cool about then letting me take my version of Padmé into new situations, so we understand who she is. We honored the original Padmé on the show, but I tried to portray her as I believe she is.

I'm quite good friends with James Arnold Taylor (Obi-Wan), so it was fun to work with him. The fans have said that they've been enjoyed the chemistry between Anakin (Matt Lanter) and Padmé. That just came naturally to us. We had great banter and we tried to make it an authentic love relationship so that you got to see these people having the same issues that real couples do. There's a strong love there. Getting to know Matt and James more, I felt a bond with them like Padmé does with Obi-Wan and Anakin in the films.

STAR WARS: THE GALAXY'S GREATEST HEROES | 121

PADMÉ AMIDALA

Dave Filoni (Supervising director, Star Wars: The Clone Wars): Padmé is one of the more complex characters we have to deal with because of who she is and the path she takes in the films. If you watch the deleted scenes materials in *Attack of the Clones*, you learn a lot more of who she is. While she's given up a lot for a public life of service, she wants a lot more for her private life. I don't think that's different from a lot of people, the way they feel about their job versus their home life.

She had a more major arc in Season Five. Padmé is always embroiled in the undertow of what's going on in the Republic, but she doesn't really know it. Like everyone, she sees it as political intrigue. But when you think about it, Padmé is the one who is actually the closest to Darth Sidious. She's the closest to what's actually going on with the evil in the galaxy, and on some level she's actually responsible for putting that evil in place. That is a very difficult thing for her, especially since she's always trying to do right, and Palpatine knows that, so he's always using her to push things a certain way for him. She's trying to do the most for the people of the Republic, but she's being deceived by someone she thinks is her friend. Even when she had a victory, for the first time in Season Five, you see she's starting to feel it's rather a Pyrrhic victory. There are things that she's getting wise to, that set up her wanting to listen to Mon Mothma later on when Mothma starts talking about Palpatine stepping down. Because if you watch the *Revenge of the Sith* deleted scenes, you see that these are not things that Padmé even wants to entertain. She supports Palpatine. It takes a bit to change her mind.

Anakin and Padmé have a more challenging relationship than people think. These two people have a lot of challenges, probably more than we know.

12 / Hayden Christensen and Natalie Portman as Anakin Skywalker and Padmé Amidala from *Attack of the Clones*.

13 / Catherine Taber's version of Padmé stays true to the cinematic version of the character.

14 / Catherine Taber— the voice of Padmé.

15 / No pushover, Padmé takes aim.

PADMÉ AMIDALA

16 / Padmé addresses the Senate.

17 / Always ready for aggressive negotiations!

" **People think Padmé is wimpy and a pacifist—no she's not! She has decorum, but when the time comes for it, she will fight.** "

▶ The show gave Padmé some classic scenes to play.

Catherine Taber: I love the scene with Jar Jar and the battle droid from "Bombad Jedi" because I think that it's hysterical. It's classic *Star Wars* humor. I love the moment in "Destroy Malevolence" when I say, "He's probably late again" because I often feel that way in real life! Anytime I have a scene with Anakin it's a lot of fun. There was a moment, I think it was in "Destroy Malevolence" too, where it's me with Obi-Wan and Anakin and it had that full-on old school *Star Wars* feel. I got to man the gunship! I would love to see more of that. I loved "Rookies"—I think everybody loved "Rookies". I have a soft spot for soldiers in general and in "Rookies" Dee [Bradley Baker] gives such heart to the clones that I just absolutely adored it. I loved "Innocents of Ryloth." I played Numa, and when I read Henry Gilroy's script, I was actually teary, and I'm not a big crier. I also love "Senate Spy." I know the actor who plays Clovis, Robin Atkin Downes very well. He has voiced a ton of game characters as well. In our scenes together it felt like I was doing a live-action show.

▶ The show was not afraid to deal with Anakin's impending struggle with the dark side.

Catherine Taber: It was important for us to start to see those glimpses of Anakin, because you don't want it to just happen in one day. I thought it was really accurate regarding how a guy would feel in those circumstances and also really accurate regarding what's going to happen to Anakin in the future. I'm a really lucky girl, what can I say? I think all of us are so close to each other and so proud of each other. The cool thing about Matt is that he's not just a pretty face; he's an amazing actor. As Anakin, he has that cockiness and confidence, but without a solid performance behind that, it wouldn't work. Matt brings that and it's not bad having him standing next to me during a romantic scene! Taber has a firm idea of which of Padmé's qualities she most admires.

Catherine Taber: I'd say Padmé is very much like me in a lot of ways. People think she's wimpy and a pacifist— no she's not! She has decorum, but when the time comes for it, she will fight. ☮

C-3PO & R2-D2

C-3PO & R2-D2

Two droids unwittingly at the center of galactic events, C-3PO and R2-D2 were given personalities by the two actors within the metal, Anthony Daniels and Kenny Baker.

Far more than just comic relief, C-3PO and R2-D2 play a vital role in the narrative across the nine *Star Wars* films. Anthony Daniels, who would go to play C-3PO in all nine theatrically released movies and numerous spin-off productions, was ready to take on the role long before filming beginning .

Anthony Daniels (C-3PO): I'd already inhabited C-3PO by proxy for six months while we were still making the costume, before we even saw a film camera—I guess something of him went inside. Being Threepio became instinctual. Some actors, some really good actors, gently talk about the art of acting. Some really bad actors really talk about the art of acting. I don't, because I actually don't really understand it, and I look at people on screen and on stage and wonder *How do you do that? How is that working, because it's brilliant.* And I can't do it.

Nobody had ever made a costume like C-3PO before *A New Hope*. Even the robot character from *Metropolis* (1927) didn't compare. And in spite of everybody's hard work, it just didn't work. I think one of the reasons the costume was slightly problematic is because our human bodies have layers of skin and fat that you can push slightly aside, but metal is very unforgiving, and it stays where it is. It wasn't the greatest experience. Of course, it made sense in the end. And the audience don't need to know about the issues of wearing a difficult costume, they just see the finished result.

Hidden away in an even less expressive costume than Daniels' was Kenny Baker.

Kenny Baker (R2-D2): I wasn't given a script. George Lucas just explained what he wanted me to do as we went along. He would direct me with a megaphone, there were no electronics to amplify outside sound inside Artoo, that's why Anthony Daniels was a little bit annoyed with me because I couldn't respond—I just couldn't hear what he was saying! Even if I had heard him, he wouldn't have been able to hear me back.

During filming, Geore Lucas had intended to dub in a different voice for C-3PO but Daniels was never in any doubt that his own voice would be used.

Anthony Daniels: I was doing the job, I was in front of the camera, I was talking. I assumed it was a given. I'd been on television, where you stand there in the light and you speak, they record your face and your voice, and you watch it on TV. Why would it be different? George left me to do the physical side totally on my own, and he could have done the vocal side totally without me, but as we know he changed his mind.

Kenny Baker (R2-D2): I didn't know how R2 was going to sound ▶

126 | STAR WARS: THE GALAXY'S GREATEST HEROES

C-3PO & R2-D2

2 /

3 /

1 / The droids reunite in a publicity shot for *Star Wars: Revenge of the Sith*. (Previous spread)

2 / Anthony Daniels tries out an early version of his costume.

3 / Kenny Baker takes a break.

4 / C-3PO hides out on the Death Star.

5 / C-3PO and R2-D2 on the greenscreen set for *Revenge of the Sith*.

▶ at all. The first time I heard Artoo 'speak' was at the premiere of the film, and I thought it was fantastic.

Kenny Baker, who passed away on 13 August, 2016, was an affable figure who bonded with his costars.

Kenny Baker (R2-D2): I went out with Alec Guinness and his wife a few times; she was a great artist and would spend a lot of the time drawing landscapes of the surrounding areas in Tunisia where we were filming.

During Episode I, Liam Neeson and I got drunk on a bottle of red wine one night after filming. There was a wrap party in the desert, it was a very good night, and the stars were out. Liam and I just sat there, drinking.

My friend Jack Purvis and I took Mark out to [small U.K. towns] Stevenage and Luton and we showed him the ropes! He was very young and he'd never been to a working man's club [a type of British social club] before. It was a whole new experience for him, and he got to see and learn a lot about life in the U.K.

Like the rest of the cast, Daniels struggled with the difficult dialogue and faced some unique challenges in order to perform.

Anthony Daniels: There are times when I didn't know how some of the others could say their lines with a straight face. If I have a bad line I can hide behind the mask. I remember particularly the line, "Listen to them R2. They're dying and it's all my fault." Even with the mask on I cringed. But the only way to do it is over the top, to ham it up, and I quite like the way it came out.

There's no room for normal gestures. We're very manual, as humans. It's part of our sense of expression, although other nations and countries do it differently. I knew that if I moved in a certain way then the costume would pinch me, but I would still do it because occasionally you had to. And the hands! Only in this very last movie do I quite deliberately pick things up that are small, because I've never been able to do that before. I learned to use what I had. In the book, I talk about one of my favorite moments in all of the movies—my confrontation with Han Solo with the Ewoks—when ▶

128 | STAR WARS: THE GALAXY'S GREATEST HEROES

6 /

▶ Han got too impertinent, and you can see the fury on C-3PO's face, but of course his face doesn't change. Liz Moore, the sculptor who created C-3PO, gave him this face that has the ability to be a very beautiful blank canvas. Without getting too technical about it, depending on its relative position to the shoulder, to the body, or whatever, and the angle, the speed of movement, you've got so many options to play with.

Kenny Baker: I thought the funniest bit was when we are in the desert and C-3PO kicks me and walks away. I said to George, "Why don't I say 'ouch!'" but he didn't seem to like the idea.

In the Podracing scene in Episode I, I was watching the race like a spectator at a tennis match with my head going left and right! Because I was doing it so quickly Artoo's head rose up a little too high. If you slow the film down

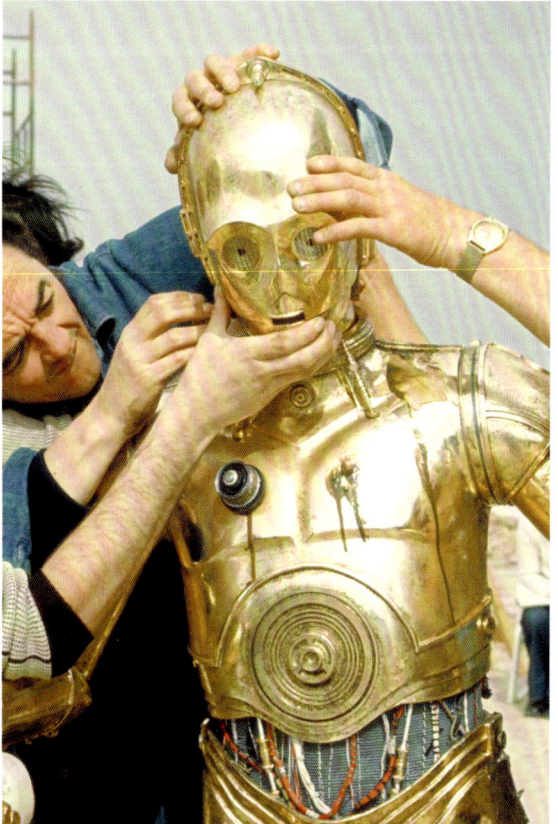

7 /

you can actually see my face in between the dome of the head and the body of Artoo!

Daniels enjoyed a shift in the dynamic in *A New Hope*'s **sequel,** *The Empire Strikes Back*.

Anthony Daniels: *The Empire Strikes Back* featured very different situations. Being partnered with Han Solo very cleverly gave C-3PO a different dynamic. As an actor you're given what to say, on the assumption that actors are stupid and they need to be told what to say and where to stand. Many of the choices are made elsewhere, in the writing room or Irvin Kershner, our director's mind. The difference, possibly, was that it was all a bit more self-conscious, whereas when we were making Episode IV, which wasn't even called Episode IV then, it was the one and only.

I felt very self-conscious that I was making a fool of myself on

130 | STAR WARS: THE GALAXY'S GREATEST HEROES

C-3PO & R2-D2

Given the rigidity of the costume walking was often a challenge.

Anthony Daniels: Anywhere that didn't have a flat, smooth floor was difficult. Anywhere with steps, that was dark, that had a low ceiling (Laughs). That was one of the horrible things, because there's a human reaction to not being able to breathe or sensing that you cannot breathe. There's an almost immediate panic reaction, and certainly that CO_2 reflex—you need to breathe, and if you have something pushing onto your diaphragm so you can't physically move it, that is scary, and it's happened to me two or three times. I would end up shouting, "Get me out, get me out!" And having people who care enough to be understanding and right there with you. There was always one, and often two people, who were my dressers from the prop department, because the suit was so technical. Absolutely looking out just for me. I gradually went set, as a character that might be thought of as being a bit wonky. But nobody was saying, "Well that's a bit rubbish, can you try something else." You have to throw yourself into it, because if you do it half-heartedly the audience absolutely won't believe you. On *Empire* we had a new director, Irvin Kershner, who, I think, found it very easy to communicate with the actors. He is very excitable. Also, the shooting schedule was a bit longer for *Empire*. The first film shot for fifteen weeks, while *Empire* shot for eighteen weeks, with part of that time in Finse in Norway. They didn't take me to Norway because my costume would literally freeze up in that kind of cold.

6 / Producer Gary Kurtz in conference with Anthony Daniels in Tunisia.

7 / Daniels gets into costume with help from the production team.

8 / Kenny Baker tries on R2-D2's feet as George Lucas and production designer John Barry look on.

9 / Anthony Daniels poses with Gary Kurtz's daughters, who played Jawas in *A New Hope*.

10 / The droids go before the camera in Tunisia. (Next spread)

C-3PO & R2-D2

> "The essence of C-3PO is C-3PO, I'm afraid. I never thought it was going to be a journey, let alone a hero's journey"

▸ through a series of people over the years, because they could only take so much. And indeed, because I've been doing this for so long, some people have retired. I was hoping that Brian Lofthouse, my dresser, would come back for the sequels, but he'd retired too.

Returning for the prequel trilogy presented a new challenge.

Anthony Daniels: C-3PO had never really left me. Although I'd done all sorts of other jobs and gigs, I had often been involved with other spin-off activities, like exhibitions and writing for *Star Wars Insider*, but I was very surprised when I met with George Lucas, who explained C-3PO's origins, his nascence, and how he'd forgotten everything. They had somebody else operating the C-3PO puppet for *The Phantom Menace*, so I was just doing the voice, but that changed in the second episode where I wore —and, to my horror, destroyed!— the puppet. It was interesting to do, to carry and perform him in a way that wasn't physically wearing the suit. But then George changed the storyline, and the puppet never appeared in the movie. C-3PO was just a rusty version instead.

In *Empire*, when C-3PO was physically blasted apart, I wore the costume in all sorts of strange ways, either with the face on the back of my head, so I was looking this way and his face was looking the other way, or with my hand up through his chest. I was literally puppeteering. We did it in so many ways. Balancing on one leg, in costume, holding a prop leg, and speaking and acting, "I'm standing here in pieces and you're having delusions of grandeur." I'm stood there with one leg in my hand and this leg up behind me, because you can really cheat with the single eye of the camera, provided you've aligned things, so you couldn't see my leg behind me. It's much easier now, with so much greenscreen. There are effects in *The Empire Strikes Back* where we created so much just by wearing the costume in a different way. And I could speak normally, and breathe!

The droids returned in 2015's *Star Wars: The Force Awakens*, which marked the beginning of a new trilogy of adventures.

Anthony Daniels: What I envy on the set is being able to improvise. You use slightly different energy in the performance than in rehearsal, but I need to know where things are. The geography of the sets is a nightmare, so I'm triangulating on anything that hopefully doesn't move. Various shots were very difficult because of effects and floor textures and so on. Finding marks is difficult, and I didn't always get it right. One day I was rehearsing with the gang, Oscar Isaac, Daisy Ridley, and John Boyega, and they're saying, "Maybe we should do this?" and suddenly I'm leaping in with this major piece of pantomime, because I rehearse exactly as I am in performance.

Reflecting on C-3PO's legacy, Daniels has a deep understanding of the droid's timeless appeal.

Anthony Daniels: The essence of C-3PO is C-3PO, I'm afraid. I never thought it was going to be a journey, certainly not a hero's journey. There was a lot of preparation in creating C-3PO, in every sense of the word, by the whole team and by me, but somehow he sort of happened. Threepio's is transparent. There's no guile, no deviousness, no mystery. He is so obvious and he always states the obvious. If everyone is cowering back as a meteor hits the window, he is the one who says, "Look, a meteor." In the wrong situation that can be very irritating, but hopefully it can be funny too. It's odd for me to realize that 40 years of my life have been spent playing C-3PO.

C-3PO, on the outside, is just who you first met back in 1977. For a lot of people, that's a very strong connection.

C-3PO's face gives the impression that he's thinking and that he cares; that he's afraid. He's always afraid. C-3PO's principal role is protocol and etiquette. Now, if there are two things that never exist in the *Star Wars* galaxy, it's protocol and etiquette. He was programmed to make people feel comfortable and for them to make other people feel comfortable. He's horrified by what he sees going on around him. He abhors space travel; he hates battles and he hates drama. He just wants to go home.

11 / Anthony Daniels on the set of Star Wars: Attack of the Clones.

REY

REY

A mysterious loner abandoned on the desolate desert planet of Jakku, Rey's journey took her across the galaxy to face a terrifying destiny.

An unknown at the time of her casting, Daisy Ridley took a chance in auditioning for the new *Star Wars* film.

Daisy Ridley (Rey): I was with some friends. Somebody said, "Did you hear *Star Wars* is coming out?" I immediately emailed my agent, and said that I really needed to audition. I don't know why; I just had this weird feeling. I wound up getting an audition and was an hour early. I was literally pacing up and down outside. I'd never been nervous like that before. It was the first time in an audition process that I felt everyone was rooting, not for me, but for the idea of an unknown actor getting the part. I knew it was a big part, but I didn't know that it would be the lead. I didn't know what Rey's journey would be and where she would end up. It was only when I read the script that I realized the enormity of things, not only for her, but her place in the whole story.

J.J. Abrams (Director, *The Force Awakens*): We looked for a long time at many people. What we were looking for was someone who felt that she was capable of everything. It's a crazy thing, but this character needed to be brought to life by an actor that didn't have limitations. We needed someone who was going to be able to be vulnerable, tough, terrified, thoughtful, sweet, and confused to take on the burden of this role and do it with authenticity. We needed someone who is able to go to this deeply emotional state and do it again and again, in some cases with brand-new actors; in other cases with actors that didn't exist at all, and in other cases, legendary actors. She needed to do all of this, and on top of everything, be an unknown. I didn't want someone who everyone knew who you had seen before. To find someone no one knew, who could do all these things, took a lot of looking.

Luckily we had our [casting directors] Nina Gold, Theo Park, and April Webster in the US working to help us find this person. It was a long search, as it needed to be. We found some great people, but it wasn't until we found Daisy that we thought we'd found the person who can do that sweet, light stuff; she has an incredible smile. She's beautiful. She could do the spirited stuff as well as the tough and emotional.

Daisy Ridley: My last audition was really amazing. A few days later, I knew I'd hear from J.J. Abrams, but my phone was broken. I didn't get the call. I didn't know what was going on. I finally got through to him, and he told me I'd be starring in *Star Wars*! I was outside a theater where my friend was in a show, of which I missed the first half while all this was going on. I remember kicking a bottle on the ground like everything had changed. But it was all the same. And then I had to watch the rest of the show. My phone died. I couldn't call anyone. I sat on the tube train [the London Underground] going home not able to tell anyone for an hour! Then, finally, I told my mum and sister. I burst the front door open and went, "I got *Star Wars*!" When I told my dad, who was asleep at the time, he just swore. That's how it happened.

The time between knowing and the announcement was so strange. I was thinking about it as if I were pregnant, like I couldn't tell anyone until the three-month mark. It was originally only a month, and it kept extending. My birthday was really hard. I sat with all my friends, and it was really hard not to say anything. As time went on, it got easier. My mum, dad, and sister knew, so I had that.

Lawrence Kasdan (Writer, *The Force Awakens*): We were very fortunate to get Daisy to play Rey because Daisy is an awesome physical specimen, yet at the same time she's a wonderful young actress who is learning all the time. You see this openness in the world,

REY

not just to the story she's in, but to acting itself. She's physically very impressive. This is a very demanding part physically. At the same time, Daisy has this incredible beauty and a wit about her that we love from the tradition of British actresses. You feel this is someone who could be in these environments and survive, and that's not easy. These are tough environments and tough situations.

It was only when Ridley won the role of Rey that the full magnitude of what being in a *Star Wars* film meant hit home.

Daisy Ridley: I remember being in the cinema and watching one of the films and being terrified. But because I was younger than the first generation of *Star Wars* fans, it wasn't such a huge thing in my life—until I got the part. But it does permeate popular culture. It's on magazine covers and it's referenced absolutely everywhere around the world.

I used to watch buses go past with movie posters on and think

4 /

that it would be really cool to see my face on the side of a bus one day!

Finding the right costume proved important for Ridley as she found the character.

Daisy Ridley: Rey begins in her own world. She goes on this crazy adventure and meets Finn and BB-8, and she finally starts to make these bonds she's never had.

We went through many versions of Rey's hair, and a few versions of her costume. When we finally decided on the hair, and I put the costume on, I could feel everyone react, that's how she should be. Everything is supposed to look like Rey put it together herself. So, the hair is the iconic three buns, which we call the three knobs! The costume is gorgeous. It's pretty, but she works in it. Everything she's got fits her perfectly. I put the costume on and I felt pretty badass!

The part demanded an intense training regime as Ridley hit the ground running.

Daisy Ridley: I started stunt training just a few weeks after I found out I had got the role. We did hand-to-hand and used boxing to warm up. J.J. wanted me to look like I work out. So, I worked on the upper body for four hours a day, four days a week for three months. Without the guys we're training with, there's just no way John Boyega and I would have gotten through Abu Dhabi! The running was so hard. It was a relief when there were explosions, because we needed a break from the running. I stopped stunt training for a while, but I kept up with the fitness training to keep the levels up. There are such long days of filming that you need the energy it brings.

Stunt-wise, we'd do warm-up and sparring, and kickboxing. Then, I'd do climbing. So, I started at a proper climbing wall, and then they had one on the stage. I really liked it. There were days when, if I slipped, my confidence was lost but it's so amazing doing something you haven't done before and feeling that you're gaining knowledge in it.

J.J. Abrams: When Daisy started doing fight training, she had such ferocity. She does this ferocious, gritting of her teeth, primal strength thing. On the one hand she's very relatable and delicate and new and innocent and, at the same time, she's insanely wise. And wildly tough. She's sort of limitless in what she can do. So, when she came in to audition,

1 / Daisy Ridley as Rey in *Star Wars: The Last Jedi* (2017).

2 / Rey and Finn, aboard the *Millennium Falcon*.

3 / The mysterious Rey, a character who had a surprising background.

4 / Rey infiltrates Starkiller Base.

5 /

5 / Finn and Rey take command of the *Millennium Falcon*!

6 / Rey unearths a mystery in the catacombs of Maz Kanata's castle.

7 / Rey brandishes the lightsaber that once belonged to Anakin and Luke Skywalker.

8 / Daisy Ridley films with BB-8 in Dubai. (Next spread)

it was clear we had someone who was going to be enormously special and make a big impact. We realized it had better be in this movie. She was too good to pass up.

Daisy Ridley: We started the staff training with a wooden stick. I don't know how I did it; the adrenaline must have kicked in on the day. I never thought I'd be able to carry on as long as I did doing the fight sequence. The staff was fun. On the day of the fight scene, I was petrified. It was the first action thing I'd done. After the fight, I felt good. I felt like all the training had been for a good reason. In training, you feel like you're pushing yourself to the limit. Then, you get on set and push further. It's an incredible feeling. I was really pleased with the training. Rey is an incredibly strong female character. I'd never climbed before; I'd never done fight training before. It's such an amazing feeling to scale a 30-foot wall, or get through a fight scene with an incredible swordsman. I feel like I held my own in those scenes, and that's an amazing feeling.

The first part of the shoot for *The Force Awakens* took place in Abu Dhabi, doubling for the desert world of Jakku.

Daisy Ridley: Abu Dhabi was really nice because we were able to go there a day early. John Boyega and I were taken around the mosque and palace, which were really lovely. We had a couple of days to get used to the heat as well. It was so hot that you could literally feel the sand burning through your shoes. But, once you give in to the heat, it's okay. You know it's consistent; it's not going to change, so there's no point in fighting it. Everyone was so well looked-after while we filmed there.

When it got to the scenes where we had to run, the hardest part was when it was a mix of hard and soft sand. That was a killer on the legs. That run was easier on the night before the last day of filming, but my lungs were really pushing it. It got hotter and hotter. You'd go from doing lots of stunt things, then to acting and intimate scenes. Towards the end of Abu Dhabi, I looked back and thought, I've really come a long way since the beginning. I could do the first few days again.

REY

The first few months of doing the job was so surreal, I can't even remember some of it. I suddenly felt part of the excitement, part of something that people were going to love and people were excited to see again. You feel you're not alone. Everyone is part of this whole thing, trying to make *Star Wars* happen again in the best possible way.

Anthony Daniels (C-3PO): Daisy really took to filming. I envy that skill and the ease that she appears to have. The effort that goes on behind it is something else, but you don't see that effort. I saw her absorb into a film set, absorbing it into her. I'm so admiring of her and John Boyega.

A key part of the plot saw Rey take flight in the *Millennium Falcon*, a scene that was given due reverence on set.

Daisy Ridley: What was so strange was that the crew was hundreds of people then suddenly it was just a few of us. It's such an iconic set and J.J. really wanted it to be perfect, so there was no mistaking what we're trying to create. It's just so big. There are moments where I was just thinking, *I'm flying the Millennium Falcon!*

Rey's always worked with machines. That's what she does and what she knows. When she winds up on the *Falcon*, she's never flown anything like it before. But she's grown up around mechanics, so she uses what she knows to get out of the situation, and start on her journey.

With Rey appearing in many scenes with Han Solo, Ridley was afforded the opportunity of working with veteran actor and *Star Wars* icon, Harrison Ford.

Daisy Ridley: When I first met Harrison Ford, we just sat down for a coffee together. He was talking about his experience in the whole thing, not just Han Solo, but the *Star Wars* saga. Then we all had dinner together, which was great.

John Boyega (Finn): Daisy is a hard worker. She's very serious and passionate about what she does. From the moment I met her, she was fixated on making this role believable and relatable. She's worked in collaboration with J.J. Abrams to make Rey loveable and soft, vulnerable, innocent, but at the same time you believe that Rey can become stern, and hard, and kick some butt! She's really strong, and it helps to have someone like that to bounce off of. We were able to collaborate in certain scenes and get the best laughs. It's been amazing not being a young lead by myself. I love the fact that it's a duo of leads. So, whatever experience we went through for the first time, it's both of us going through it. In real life and in the movie.

The theme of family is one very important to Ridley.

Daisy Ridley: Rey begins in her own world. She goes on this crazy adventure and meets Finn and BB-8, and she finally starts to make these bonds she's never had. The family theme translates everywhere. Even on set, it felt like a family. It's that feeling of bonding. Because Rey is trying to find her place in this world in the same way I was trying to find my place in the world, the similarities were really nice. I felt so welcomed and taken in, and people seemed to care how I felt, which translates into the Rey thing as well. She suddenly has these people who care about her.

The final scene of the film was shot on the island of Skellig Michael, off the coast of Ireland.

Daisy Ridley: I do remember one of the most touching moments was at the end, because I looked ▶

REY

9 / Rey arrives as her friends in the Resistance fights for their lives on Crait.

10 / Rey uses the Force to elude the First Order.

11 / Rey and Kylo Ren destroy a piece of the past in the heat of battle.

12 / Rey on the remote island of Ahch-To.

▶ back and just couldn't believe everything that had happened over the many months since I started on the film. I couldn't help but recall all the incredible amounts of hard work, passion, and energy that have been given so graciously by the cast and crew. It all just paid off.

I found the last day of filming to be the most emotional, but it was also the most exciting. I'm part Irish, so to be in Ireland was very exciting; and the approach to Skellig is unlike anything I've ever seen. Firstly, I'd never been in a helicopter before. The weather was stunning. It's just one of the most amazing places I've ever been. But it was tough. There were many steps to climb. But Colin Anderson, our incredible Steadicam operator, was walking backwards up the stairs with a 100-pound camera, so the whole thing was pretty awe-inspiring. I was sick on the last day, so I was feeling a bit awful, but it kind of helped with the emotion that Rey is feeling in the scene.

For *Star Wars: The Last Jedi*, Rey's wardrobe suggested a darker path in her journey.

Michael Kaplan (Costume designer): Rey's finding her inner strength, but she's still Rey. There is enough of a change to move her, and her story, along. Having been dressed for the desert in *The Force Awakens*, it made sense that she would adopt a poncho now that she was heading for a place with cooler, rainier weather. The colors have changed too for the same environmental reasons: while the pale colors worked on Jakku, darker colors seemed appropriate for where she is going.

Ridley felt a sense of ownership over Rey.

Daisy Ridley: I realized what *Star Wars* might be to people. I hoped that people would love it. I felt like I was working with my film family. Every day was fun. I haven't had one day where I didn't enjoy it. There are moments when I think how many people love *Star Wars*, and it's scary trying to fit into that world that people know so well and love so much. It was nerve-wracking thinking what Rey might represent to these people and whether they would like her or not.

Ridley was very keen that the cast's enthusiasm would translate to the audience.

Daisy Ridley: I'd love for people to feel the same way we do working on the *Star Wars* films. There's such a good feeling about them and what we're doing and the characters that are being made and formed in front of our eyes. I'd love for the audience to understand each of the characters' stories and connect with the new characters, and I hope that their ▶

144 | STAR WARS: THE GALAXY'S GREATEST HEROES

REY

love for the old characters returns even more than before. I'd love for people to leave the cinema thinking, aside from all the action and the fights, that it's an incredible story of people finding their place in a world.

Rian Johnson (Director, *Star Wars: The Last Jedi*): Daisy is an extraordinary young actor, bringing incredible depth and emotion that she brought to the role of Rey. I discovered that so much that people respond to in the character of Rey comes from Daisy: her tenacity, her bravery, her humor, her depth, so many things that make little kids want to be Rey, those things are Daisy.

Over the course of the trilogy, Ridley had scenes with Mark Hamill and Adam Driver.

Daisy Ridley: Mark's a talker and Adam isn't. Mark has lived a crazy life. A lot of his life has been influenced by Star Wars, and he's so well-known for it. He's older; he's a father, so his energy is steadier. Adam is incredible. He has this amazing depth of emotion.

Luke Skywalker embodies so much of everyone. Everyone starts out on a path; then circumstances change, and things happen, and you go to a new path. The thing that's always with him is the good. He's the good against the evil. He's looking out for Leia and Han Solo too. So, he's got other people's best interests at heart. The choices he makes are positively affecting, not only him, but the people around him as well. I think that's what so many people do in life and that's probably why I feel like that. He's someone I can relate to. I really like the line from *The Empire Strikes Back* when Yoda tells Luke that he has to go in a dark cave. Luke asks Yoda, "What's in there?" And Yoda says, "Only what you take with you." That brings everything together; the idea that everything you have inside you hopefully will lead to good things. Luke, even at the end, hoped for the best in his father. So you have to give it to him that his hope held out.

Ridley feels that the saga offers important life lessons.

Daisy Ridley: I think in fifty years time, I'll look back and really realize the life lessons that I learned from this part of the journey as kind of a whole. So hopefully, I'll learn some more life lessons on the way. There are lessons to be strong and be thoughtful and take care, and realize how you're affecting other people. Learn and grow and don't be scared if things are offered to you that you're not sure about, but that may change your life. Jump in feet first. Take everything you can and appreciate every day. Appreciate the people around you who support you and never feel on your own, because you never are.

13 /

14 /

13 / Rey stands amidst the celebrations during the Festival of Ancestors on Pasaana.

14 / Rey witnessing a chilling possible future if she embraces her darker instincts.

15 / After refusing to follow her grandfather's adoption of the dark side, Rey adopts the name "Skywalker."

FINN

FINN

A stormtrooper who goes against the orders of his superior, FN-2187 joins forces with Poe Dameron to stage a daring escape from the First Order. Played by the charismatic actor John Boyega, the newly renamed Finn embarks on a journey into the heart of his former enemy.

A unique character in the saga, John Boyega was very familiar with the saga from childhood.

John Boyega (Finn): I was born in 1992, so I grew up on the prequels, and then my dad told me that I should go back and watch the originals because that rounds up the whole Anakin and Luke Skywalker story. So I went back and watched the originals and thought they were amazing. Every actor captured our imaginations and it was definitely an artistic influence for actors, directors, and everybody in the entertainment field, from visual effects to everybody that makes the magic happen.

Return of the Jedi is my favorite film, because you find Luke Skywalker at a very vulnerable time. In the first film he was learning who he is and learning about this special world that's out there that he never knew about. *Return of the Jedi* is a great mix of drama, comedy, and somewhat expands the universe in terms of the Ewoks and other creatures that you find in the movie. It's my favorite because it's the establishment of each character at a different point in their lives. You see the whole story from a different point of view. I always saw the first two films as from the point of view of R2-D2 and C-3PO. I only cared about these droids. These droids are just being exchanged, and passed around, and the story is told from their viewpoint. But, *Return of the Jedi* is fixated on Luke Skywalker's story and he's becoming the top Jedi on the streets right now and that was really cool to me.

Casting for *Star Wars: The Force Awakens* involved a long and involved process.

John Boyega: I got a call about the auditions for *Star Wars* and my agent told me that J.J. Abrams wanted to meet with me and put me on tape for the role. I didn't know what part I was going up for and I hadn't read the script, so I took a train into central London, met J.J., spoke about the role, and then did the scenes. It was two scenes; I practiced it a few times, and then we put it on tape. It was quite the experience because it was nerve-wracking knowing that it was *Star Wars*, but not knowing the specifics of the part. After that it was recall after recall, then a screen test with Chewbacca came, which was exciting. Then, I got the call to say that I had got the part, and that was after seven months of extreme auditioning!

From the get-go, they specified that it was a male leading role. *Star Wars* is an ensemble cast, so we have lots of leads that create the narrative, and I didn't know that Finn was so central to the story. I only found that out halfway through the audition process when J.J. said, "You're the guy. You know that, right?" I was like, "Ahh! Okay, it's time to get the acting chops together and do something!"

Prior to getting the part, I had been at a premiere for another film I had done, and my mind was definitely more fixated on whether I'd receive the part or not. I remember being on the red carpet and it had leaked that I was up for the *Star Wars* part. So, there were various media outlets asking if I was up for *Star Wars*. I said, "I haven't heard anything, but if J.J. Abrams wants me to be in *Star Wars*, that would be amazing." The next day, I got an email from J.J. asking where I was. I told him I was at home and he asked if I could get to a little café in Mayfair, London. I hopped in a cab, drove down, and saw J.J. in the café by himself, drinking a cup of tea. We had a brief conversation and he asked me whether I was ▶

FINN

ready. He asked me if would be interested in working out and training, both as an actor and physically. He asked me if I realized how big the responsibility would be. I said, "Yeah, I'll be fine. I'll do anything." Then, he told me I was the new star in *Star Wars*. Everything stopped.

I noticed everything. I noticed how many sugar cubes were in this little cup on the table. All the time it was going through my head, he just said I'm the new star in *Star Wars*. I was willing myself to breathe. Then J.J. raised a cup of water and said, "Congratulations." I was ecstatic. It was probably the happiest day of my life. I walked all around London just in a dreamland. This felt different. I've received calls for roles that I fought for before, but this not only felt like a triumph for me as an actor, but a day that felt like I was a part of history and that just made me really, really happy.

However, winning the role of Finn was not something that the exuberant actor could initially talk about.

John Boyega: We were told to keep quiet; we couldn't tell any family or friends. No one knew about it. Obviously, there was no press release and it was really hard just going through normal life without saying that I was cast in *Star Wars*! But I was really excited that the picture came out with all of us at the read-through. It was really historical. It was amazing. I didn't even tell my parents! They found out the day of the read-through because I was told specifically to keep it quiet.

The London-born actor was unfazed when asked to perform the character with an American accent.

John Boyega: Doing an American accent is quite interesting. I remember auditioning and there were talks about whether Finn was going to be doing an American accent, or a British accent. I was very happy that they chose an American accent because one of my favorite characters is Han Solo, and Han Solo has this very boyish, charismatic American accent and it makes him sound like he's king of the world. The accent does help me channel that energy a bit. It's great for Finn, and it does help with making him funny and relatable.

Boyega has nothing but praise for his two-time collaborator, J.J. Abrams.

John Boyega: J.J. Abrams is an actor's director. He understands the balance between the technical and the artistic. He gets the best out of his crew and his cast. Until we reach a balance, he won't be satisfied. That's what I love about J.J. Also, J.J. is a *Star Wars* fan. He's clued up about *Star Wars* and was very energetic on the set. He's a very vibrant young man! From an actor's perspective, he gave me the best notes in terms of a scene and helped me get the best out of my character. It was fun working with him.

J.J.'s influence was evident when I first read the script [for *The Force Awakens*]. Especially with Finn, because Finn is charismatic like J.J.; fun, very funny, and very real. That's a part of J.J. that he's put in Finn. But also it connects to the original *Star Wars*, where there was danger, but it wasn't like, drama-danger, it's *Star Wars* danger; it's exciting and thrilling.

The physical demands of the role called for Boyega to embarking on a strenuous training regime.

John Boyega: For a role in a film like *Star Wars*, there's a lot of action and J.J. is great at doing action both in space and on the ground. As actors, we needed to learn some hand-to-hand combat and how to use the lightsabers, so I was involved in over seven months of training. There was

1 / John Boyega as stormtrooper FN-2187 aka Finn in *Star Wars: The Force Awakens*. (Previous spread)

2 / Finn settles an old score at Takodana.

3 / Finn goes up against Kylo Ren.

4 / Manning the *Millennium Falcon*'s gunning station during the escape from Jakku.

5 / Boyega and Daisy Ridley share a joke while filming a sequence that was ultimately deleted. (Next spread)

2 /

3 /

FINN

actually a lot of John Williams' *Star Wars* music coming from the speakers in the gym. I would do some intervals and run and do some cardio, skipping, boxing, weight training, all that kind of stuff. When we started filming, I felt like I was really ready.

The combat training was pretty serious stuff. Our lightsabers were really heavy, so you do get a sense of the power that's coming out of this weapon and it does really do something to you, but you do have to be strong and you have to have skill. But it was been fun doing the stunt training because I've always wanted to swing a lightsaber. We were actually working with wooden sticks for a long time to keep safe and get used to the movement and to learn the choreography.

The actor's first scenes were shot in the scorching heat of Abu Dhabi, doubling for the desert world of Jakku.

John Boyega: Abu Dhabi, in the heat, was quite the experience. Going out there and being in this environment—huge desert, loads of props, a big set, and obviously J.J. Abrams with his enthusiasm and his energy coming in was just amazing. Just looking around and taking it all in and saying, "I am here. We are about to film this movie." I knew it was going to be an experience I would never forget.

The actor formed a close bond with co-star Daisy Ridley, who played Rey in the film.

John Boyega: Daisy Ridley and I met during the audition process, and it was important for us to know each other so that we could have good chemistry on screen. Ever since then we've just bonded and we had a great time. It's funny because we're both going through this same experience of being in a picture that's huge, and being on something of this scale is new to both of us. We're kind of holding

FINN

▶ each other's hand through this experience, and we've been having fun! Cracking jokes and singing nice sing-along songs every morning, which everyone else doesn't like, but we do our thing! Daisy and I get along on screen and off screen, so what you will see in the movie, in terms of our rhythm, in terms of our banter, is real off-screen. When J.J. was going through the script with us, he made some tweaks based on our relationship and the rhythm of the way we talk to each other. It's great that's been implemented in the movie, because people will feel that these two strangers, who've come from two different worlds, but are somewhat the same, are bonding and that there's a real friendship between them. When you believe in characters that have great chemistry, you buy into the reality of it. You care about the characters. So, it's been wonderful working with Daisy, and having this real chemistry on screen.

Daisy Ridley (Rey): John's like an annoying little brother. He's always telling me to shut up because I sing all the time! It's so great how well we get on. In Abu Dhabi we didn't have a chance to really meet, and that relationship wasn't there at first. But since we started filming in London, and building that relationship in the scenes, it's easy. It's not hard to find it with someone you get on with. It's a chemistry thing. As it went on, we're just like brother and sister. We get on really well. We're both incredibly silly. With the adults on set you can feel they're thinking, *Oh we've got two children here!*

Filming at Pinewood Studios proved to be an eye-opening experience for the actor as he found himself working with all manner of performers, both human and otherwise...

John Boyega: When I walked onto the set, it took my breath away. It was amazing. The sets matched ▶

FINN

FINN

what they were back in the first three original *Star Wars* movies. It's easier to act when everything around you is physical, and you can play with some things. It's the *Star Wars* magic and that's something George Lucas started.

I had fun surrounded by the creatures. I am a big creature-feature fan, and I love physical effects. I love the creatures being right there in my face. We had a great team that did the puppetry on these creatures. It was hilarious, because when the camera's not rolling they still stay in it, so the animatronics are still going, the puppetry's still going, so you find yourself having conversations with several different species you've never met before!

The first live-action *Star Wars* film in a decade carried an enormous weight of expectation.

John Boyega: There's something amazing about the new generation characters in Star Wars. They are obviously younger, and less experienced, and they don't know about themselves as much as the other characters do. They don't have an established view of the galaxy, and they are learning. Finn is definitely the physical representation of the young generation when it comes to the *Star Wars* universe. *Star Wars* has a huge following, but there is a small percentage of young people who haven't been introduced to the *Star Wars* universe, or who are more into the Legends stories, but don't know how to relate to the movies. Finn is their direct link. He doesn't know what's going on and is freaked out by droids and aliens. I think the audience will enjoy a relatable character and his experiences.

The Force Awakens sequel, Star Wars: The Last Jedi, and its sequel, The Rise of Skywalker gave Finn an increasingly important role in the story.

John Boyega: [*The Last Jedi*'s director, Rian Johnson] had a strong attention to detail, and specific and honest notes, along with strong sense of collaboration. I feel the best directors know how to collaborate, and he did just that.

Finn is more aware about his part in this story, that he has matured and become more of a fighter. It's still the case that there are some loose ends in terms of his character development.

The Last Jedi developed a relationship between Finn and fellow rebel, Rose.

John Boyega: Finn's relationship with Rose is about two people who are thrown together by circumstance and fate. As a consequence, Finn and Rose make a really good team.

Boyega views his work on the *Star Wars* films as life-changing.

John Boyega: *Star Wars* has been such a major part of my life these last few years. It wasn't until I got a role in *Star Wars* that my life changed at an amazing speed, and it's been great. What has stood out the most is the collaboration I've shared with all the amazing individuals who have been a part of creating these movies. I've made friends and become part of a big family, and that's a major thing to let go of. As for Finn, I feel good about him. He went from being part of something oppressive to being thought of as a hero.

6 / Finn as seen in *Star Wars: The Rise of Skywalker*.

7 / Finn, Poe Dameron, and Kaydel Ko Connix escape from the ruined outpost on Crait.

JYN ERSO

Felicity Jones' performance in *Rogue One: A Star Wars Story* (2016) saw a new kind of hero make her mark on the *Star Wars* galaxy, as Jyn Erso embarked on a deadly mission.

The first standalone *Star Wars* movie featured a disparate team uniting around Jyn Erso, a young woman who embarks on a mission with high stakes both for herself and the galaxy.

Gareth Edwards (Director, *Rogue One: A Star Wars Story*): We talked about the fact that Jyn isn't just a woman—she's a person. We always tried to treat her like that. I wanted to make a character that I would want to be. Not to fancy her or want to marry her, but want to be her. Jyn is just a cool person. We tried to make the film in such a way where the issue of boy or girl never came into it.

The actress Felicity Jones, acclaimed for her roles in *The Theory of Everything* (2014), *The Invisible Woman* (2013), and *A Monster Calls* (2016), was cast as Jyn Erso.

Felicity Jones (Jyn Erso): I grew up with my older brother and lots of boy cousins. I remember them all sitting around watching it earnestly as I came in through the door. I remember that incredible title sequence from *Star Wars: A New Hope* (1977) going up the screen. But, I have to say, my affection for *Star Wars* came from watching it in preparation for *Rogue One* and going back to watch those early films and becoming rather obsessed with it.

Kathleen Kennedy (Producer): *The Force Awakens* and *Rogue One* having strong female characters is very indicative of what we're talking about doing going forward. We are finding diversity in our cast, whether it be ethnic diversity or male/female,

> "Jyn knows where she came from."

representation. We need to make sure that the diversity in our society is reflected in the stories that we tell.

Felicity Jones: The thing about Jyn is that everyone should relate to her. It doesn't matter whether she's female or male. She's not just tough; like all human beings she can also be vulnerable.

Gareth Edwards: You can just hang the camera on Felicity and not say a word, and you can feel her having a million different thoughts. You get interested in what she's thinking and what's going on. She can be very observant within a scene. It doesn't always have to be about her directly, but we're experiencing it through her. She just has that knack for pulling you in.

Jones was interested in the character's sole focus on destiny rather than her past.

Felicity Jones: I feel there's one major difference between Jyn and other *Star Wars* heroes [such as] Rey and Luke. She's not a character asking, "Who am I and where did I come from?" Rather, Jyn knows where she came from, and that propels the story and her journey. At the beginning of the film, she's very much a maverick. She's her own person. She's someone who doesn't know how to keep to the rules and is always pushing the boundaries.

For the first time in *Star Wars* history, the main protagonist was not a Force user.

Felicity Jones: I wanted Jyn to be as human as possible. She's strong when she needs to be, she's incredibly determined and she has to be tough when she doesn't feel it. Gareth made everything feel as real as possible. He wants authenticity and that's hard work with harsh conditions, continual rain, sand being kicked in your face, but he wants an audience to feel that they are actually there and that's so important.

JYN ERSO

2 /

▶ Costume was important for the character with Jones approving of the design choices made.

Felicity Jones: The costume was one of my favorite parts of Jyn. We looked at a lot of different references. We liked Japanese influences, so Jyn's undershirt was based on a Japanese design. It was important that Jyn had a toughness and strength but rooted in femininity. We didn't want her to be just dressing like a guy. She needed her own identity and her own way of doing things that came through her clothes.

Jyn Erso embarks on her mission with a team of soldiers, including the jaded rebel, Cassian Andor (Diego Luna).

1 / Felicity Jones as Jyn Erso in a publicity shot for *Rogue One: A Star Wars Story*. (Previous spread)

2 / Jyn Erso engages the enemy on Eadu.

3 / Jyn's relationship with her father lies at the center of the movie's narrative.

4 / Jyn addresses the Rebel Alliance.

5 / Jyn and her team —the "Rogue One" of the film's title.

3 /

4 /

JYN ERSO

Felicity Jones: Subconsciously throughout the film, Jyn is putting together a team. She is suspicious of Cassian. She's put in this position of going on a mission with someone she's never met before in her life. She's naturally cautious about him. They're both similar in that they're both headstrong. They're not immediately best friends, which is fun to play. But they go through so much together. They can't help but create this bond. There's a true friendship, and true respect, by the end of the film. They really earn each other's affection.

When she comes across Bodhi Rook (Riz Ahmed) she doesn't realize straight away that there is a connection between them. Jyn is very empathetic and doesn't like to see anyone suffering, so she instinctively wants to help him and that is the start of their bond and friendship.

JYN ERSO

8 /

▶ A pivotal bond in the film is formed when the partisan leader Saw Gerrera (Forest Whitaker) rescues the young Jyn Erso.

Felicity Jones: Saw Gerrera is the closest person that Jyn has to a parental figure. Not having her parents around, she's had to learn to be very self-reliant, and Saw Gerrera has shown her that not only does she have to rely on herself but she has to have strong convictions and be able to defend those convictions. When Jyn and Saw meet, there's an incredible connection between them, a closeness and a bond. But, also, there's friction. You can see Jyn is trying to forge her own way. Forest is so brilliant technically, but is also the most soulful human being I've ever met in my entire life. He brought such humanity to the character and such complexity. I feel speechless talking about him. I had a fantastic time working with him.

Although Jones only played Jyn Erso in one film and voiced the character in three episodes of the *Forces of Destiny* **micro-series, Kathleen Kennedy believes she is an important character in the** *Star Wars* **history.**

Kathleen Kennedy: Felicity is such a brilliant actress and brings a sense of gravitas and importance to everything she does, yet there's a real whimsy to her, too. She has a great smile, a wonderful sense of humor, and was fantastic to work with. She shows the strength and empowerment that we're looking for in female characters in *Star Wars*. One day I hope we don't even have to talk about that because it will just be accepted that the female leads in *Star Wars* are as important as their male counterparts and recognized beyond gender for playing a great role.

6 / Erso and Cassian Andor on Jedha. (Previous spread)

7 / Jones' performance was acclaimed by Kathleen Kennedy as conveying the strength and empowerment essential to *Star Wars* female characters.

8 / The rebels don the clothes of the enemy in order to infiltrate the base on Scarif.

POE DAMERON

POE DAMERON

Poe Dameron's instinctive skill as a pilot often put him at odds with the leaders of the Resistance, including General Organa. Originally due to be killed off during *The Force Awakens*' first act, Oscar Isaac's fiery fighter ace became a popular hero of the sequel trilogy.

For the acclaimed actor, whose career encompasses roles in films as diverse as *Drive* (2011), *Robin Hood* (2010), and *Inside Llewyn Davis* (2013) the role of Poe Dameron began with a step into the unknown.

Oscar Isaac (Poe Dameron): I got a call to come and meet J.J. Abrams in Paris and I showed up without any information as to exactly what it was about. I had a vague feeling that it was about *Star Wars*, but even that was a bit under wraps. J.J, Kathleen Kennedy, and Lawrence Kasdan told me about the film and the role that they were interested in me playing. I just tried to stay cool and stay calm and listen and take it in. But really my reaction was utter excitement and disbelief that this was actually happening.

Poe Dameron joined Finn and Rey, forming a triumvirate of stars across the trilogy.

Oscar Isaac: J.J. put the trio together, and I think it definitely helped capture some of the spirit from the original trilogy. There's a dynamic between the three characters that's great. In as much as these movies are about the Skywalker saga, for me doing these movies has also been the saga of me meeting John Boyega (Finn) and to experience this adventure with him. He has such a beautiful heart and is such a beautiful person. I definitely admire him. My first screen test for *The Force Awakens* was with John, in the TIE fighter. And we've been back-to-back ever since.

Isaac was pleased with Poe Dameron's role within that trio as it developed over the filming.

Oscar Isaac: The nuance of the characters and how they interact with each other, and what they say, and how they respond and how that reveals who the characters are is interesting to play with. So any suggestions I might have come from a place of how those things get affected and how they can be highlighted. That was an interesting thing with playing Poe; It's a specific color that he adds to the film. It's one that's energetic. There's almost an old-school Cary Grant in *His Girl Friday* (1940) kind of speed to it, and that's something that J.J. really liked.

Isaac found that making a *Star Wars* film was unlike anything he had experienced in his career to date.

Oscar Isaac: What's great is that this is being done with no cynicism. It's being done open-hearted and with such love and enthusiasm from everybody, starting with J.J. that I think it's going to be infectious. You can feel that coming off the screen; just the love of *Star Wars* and the love of these stories and being able to add new ones to the legacy. J.J. has been doing it exactly how you ▶

POE DAMERON

would want these films to be handled. Obviously, they mean so much to everyone. Everyone has ownership over them. Everyone wants them to be their thing. That's always a difficult and scary thing because everyone has a very specific idea of what it should be. But I think when you approach it with this much love and generosity, that stuff becomes less important. You see that this is someone who loves it so much and has found people that love it just as much and who want to make it special and beautiful. It has defied what I could have expected. I think that's because of J.J. Abrams, who has allowed people to feel ownership over it. You're not just being allowed to come into this world, this is *your* world and you get to add to it. You get to really live out these characters and be part of this world. I think that's been so generous of him. And being on set and interacting with droids and aliens, the actual ships, and hundreds of extras infuses you with the energy of the scene.

Star Wars: The Last Jedi director Rian Johnson was enthused by Isaac's charisma.

Rian Johnson (Director, *Star Wars: The Last Jedi*): Oscar Isaac is a reincarnation of my favorite old movie stars; he has that old school magnetism paired with insane acting chops. Poe is a straight-up, good-guy hero, and although he gets put through the wringer in this film, because of Oscar you never lose faith that he's going to come out the other end all the better for it.

Oscar Isaac: [*The Last Jedi* explores themes of] what it means to resist and what it means to win, with some very truthful messages about power and the nature of power and those seeking power and how easily it can go one way or another. It's finding out what a hero is. What it is to be a hero and what it is to be a leader. You get more specific and find the nuance in the situation, and

1 / Oscar Isaac as reckless X-wing ace Poe Dameron. (Previous spread)

2 / Filming the daring TIE fighter escape sequence with John Boyega.

POE DAMERON

how you can explore those themes. It's a war. They're in the midst of a war; it is life and death, and the decisions made affect so many. Especially on Poe's side, which is focused on the Resistance.

For 2019's *The Rise of Skywalker*, Isaac was reunited with his *The Force Awakens* director J.J. Abrams.
Oscar Isaac: There were times J.J. would do one long scene in one-take. Sometimes it would be quite complicated, with multiple people in the scene, and he would choreograph the whole thing. And what's wonderful about that as an actor is that it's up to you to dictate the rhythm. When you shoot a scene all in one take, the actors get to really have some fun, which enables a bit of improvisation. Although J.J. had this incredible task of bringing closure to a saga more than 40 years in the making, he still had a looseness about him and a curiosity to try different things. He just had this unrelenting vision about what he wanted to accomplish, not to mention incredible energy and drive. That was really exhilarating.

***The Rise of Skywalker* saw Dameron fulfil his destiny as he stepped forward to lead the Resistance.**

Oscar Isaac: Poe finds himself inheriting a Resistance that is on the brink of collapse. He feels completely lost, and he even begins to wonder if there's really anything to lead at this point. But Poe is reminded about family and friends and not being alone. And he rallies behind those ideas and pushes the others to continue to move forward.

3 / Dameron and the Resistance plot their next move on D'Qar.

4 / Tortured by Kylo Ren, Poe Dameron was not originally intended to survive the first act of *The Force Awakens*.

5 / The saga charts Poe Dameron's journey from rogue pilot to Resistance leader.

WICKET W. WARRICK

WICKET W. WARRICK

<u>After responding to an ad requesting short actors to audition for a part in what what later be revealed to be the new *Star Wars* film, *Return of the Jedi*, 11 year old Warwick Davis ended up playing the role of Wicket, one of Endor's warrior Ewoks.</u>

Warwick Davis was a fan of the saga prior to winning the role of Wicket.

Warwick Davis (Wicket W. Warrick): I was one of the youngest performers to be in the original trilogy, so for them I guess it was something quite new for the rest of the cast and crew. I was like a fan had won a part in the film. Initially I was going around like a tourist. My Mom and Dad had their camera out and were taking a few photographs, but it wasn't a thing that bothered anybody. I've got a few snaps of me in the Ewok costume and in the wardrobe department that you wouldn't get now; you're not allowed anywhere near there with a camera anymore because word spreads so quickly on the internet. Back then you could have shouted it from the rooftops and no one would have listened. It was a very different time, but one that still required an element of secrecy. It wasn't about it being reported —it was about the set being invaded, or the trash being gone through by fans trying to find the filming locations.

Although he found fame as Wicket, Davis was not orginally cast as the distinctive Ewok.

Warwick Davis: I was always in there as an Ewok. I forget what number—we were all numbered— but I was one of forty Ewoks that were put together for the scene in the village. We filmed for about six weeks during a very cold winter, and I remember one day they wanted some still photos, but not in the costume: just as me, my head and shoulders. I was on set and I was half in the costume. I didn't question why they did it, but I'd been chosen— along with a few other actors including Jack Purvis [Teebo], Mike Edmonds [Logray], I think Malcolm Dixon [one of the Ewok warriors], and Kenny Baker [R2-D2]—to go to America to join the U.S. contingent of Ewoks to film the Battle of Endor sequences. What I didn't know at the time was that photograph was for my passport, because I didn't have one. They went ahead and organized the passport for me, and then sprang the surprise that I'd be going to America to carry on this great adventure that I'd started in London.

But I still wasn't Wicket; at that point I was an Ewok that had been featured a bit, particularly during one of the establishing shots in the village. There was a main area in the village, where the fires were and where we tried to roast Han, and I remember Artoo was leaning against a hut tied to wooden poles. He'd been released by Teebo and he was sort of standing there, and during one shot I thought, *Hang on a minute, I'm going to wander over and have a look at this, because as an Ewok I think I'd be pretty curious about this new addition to the village*. So, I went over and was interacting, and I think the director, Richard Marquand, noticed and gave me a little featured moment. Then they encouraged me to keep on doing ▶

WICKET W. WARRICK

what I was doing, but all I was doing was being Warwick Davis, looking through the eyes of this character, thinking, *How would I respond to these situations?*

I was using the inquisitive nature of my dog at the time, who used to tilt his head from side to side when he heard a strange sound. I thought it was really endearing and he looked very cute when he did that, so I started doing the same thing as Wicket, and it looked very endearing on an Ewok as well. When you're in those suits, all you have to perform with is your body. You can't make facial expressions—all you have are your arms, your legs, and the orientation of your body to create the expression or the mood that you want to convey. I guess even at 11 years-old I was thinking that way.

Davis has warm memories of the distinctly chilly Elstree set.

Warwick Davis: I remember it being very cold; it was a very cold winter when we were shooting in the UK. We would come out of the soundstage at Elstree. There were two soundstages next to each other; one with the Ewok village set and the other with the *Millennium Falcon*. When you walked between the stages there was a sheltered area. You'd not get rained on, but the ends were open to the elements, so the wind would blow down. We'd walk down in the Ewok suits, steaming, and a lovely cold draught would blow down this alleyway and keep us cool.

On the set there were some log cabins where we'd sit and relax while waiting for the next set-up. Back in those days they'd use incense to give a haze to the atmosphere and the smell was quite overwhelming. If I smell incense now, I can be transported right back to the Ewok village.

Working in those conditions was pretty oppressive. It was hot for the crew, let alone the Ewoks!

WICKET W. WARRICK

1 / Ewok warrior Wicket as played by Warwick Davis. (Previous spread)

2 / A 13 year old in paradise! Warwick takes a break on set with Jabba the Hutt.

3 / A production sketch of Wicket by art director Joe Johnston.

4 / Wicket as observed in his natural habitat.

6 / Wicket has a fateful encounter with Leia. The two would bond offscreen as well as onscreen, with Carrie Fisher bringing milk and cookies to the set for her young co-star.

5 / R2-D2 meets Wicket. Note that Davis' eyes can be seen through the costume. (Next spread)

WICKET W. WARRICK

> "You've got to be willing to use your imagination but also to interpret the scene for yourself."

▶ Then you've got the smoke and the lights, and you're working 20 feet off the ground! It was a difficult environment to be in and there wasn't much room with all the equipment and crew. It was quite a challenge to shoot.

Davis found George Lucas' famously laid back style of directing suited his own style of performance.

Warwick Davis: George Lucas's style of directing, certainly as far as I was concerned, was like, *If you can start over there and be there by the end, it's kind of up to you what you do in the middle.* I like that as an actor, because you're employed to act, and I don't expect to have my hand held the whole way through it. I think you've got to be willing to use your imagination, but also interpret the scene for yourself.

Following *Return of the Jedi*, Davis returned as Wicket in two movies made for TV—*The Ewok Adventure* (1984) and *Ewoks: The Battle for Endor* (1985).

Warwick Davis: When we made the two Ewok TV movies, they changed Wicket's costume somewhat. In improving it (as they thought), they based Wicket's feet around a pair of trainers, so I could put my feet in, do the laces up, and then over the top of it was the molded Ewok foot with toes and fur. If I lifted up my foot, you could quite clearly see the tread of the trainer underneath. The feet I'd been used to while doing *Return of the Jedi* were made of foam rubber; the whole foot was. It was like wearing a very bulbous slipper with an inch thick sole.

7 / Wicket joins the droids as the rebels raid the Imperial bunker on Endor.

8 / Cindel Towani and Wicket in *Ewoks: The Battle for Endor.*

9 / Davis' performance as Wicket was the springboard for a career that saw the actor play the title role in Lucasfilm's *Willow* (1988).

As I walked it was like being on a really rounded cushion, so it gave me a very distinctive walk. Wearing these made me feel like the character. When I wore the new shoes, I didn't feel anything like the character anymore. It changed the way I walked and it was completely different. It's amazing that something as simple as a pair of shoes can be so important!

For the 2011 reissue of the film, a digitial blink was added to the otherwise stoic Wicket's features.

Warwick Davis: Originally, the only movement on that face was my tongue. It was an unusual step to have one of the main characters be so expressionless, but it worked, probably due to my superb acting! To add blinking is building on my performance.

STAR WARS LIBRARY

STAR WARS: THE EMPIRE STRIKES BACK: THE 40TH ANNIVERSARY SPECIAL EDITION

STAR WARS: THE MANDALORIAN GUIDE TO SEASON ONE

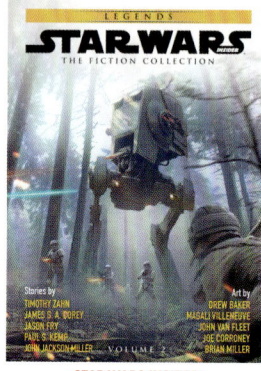
STAR WARS INSIDER: THE FICTION COLLECTION VOLUME 2

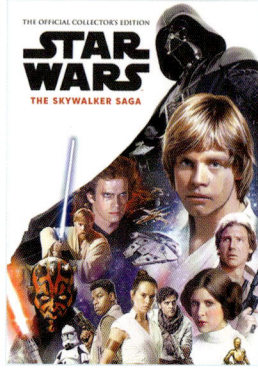
STAR WARS: THE SKYWALKER SAGA THE OFFICIAL collector's edition

- **ROGUE ONE: A STAR WARS STORY** THE OFFICIAL COLLECTOR'S EDITION
- **ROGUE ONE: A STAR WARS STORY** THE OFFICIAL MISSION DEBRIEF
- **STAR WARS: THE LAST JEDI** THE OFFICIAL COLLECTOR'S EDITION
- **STAR WARS: THE LAST JEDI** THE OFFICIAL MOVIE COMPANION
- **STAR WARS: THE LAST JEDI** THE ULTIMATE GUIDE
- **SOLO: A STAR WARS STORY** THE OFFICIAL COLLECTOR'S EDITION
- **SOLO: A STAR WARS STORY** THE ULTIMATE GUIDE
- **THE BEST OF STAR WARS INSIDER** VOLUME 1
- **THE BEST OF STAR WARS INSIDER** VOLUME 2
- **THE BEST OF STAR WARS INSIDER** VOLUME 3
- **THE BEST OF STAR WARS INSIDER** VOLUME 4
- **STAR WARS:** LORDS OF THE SITH
- **STAR WARS:** HEROES OF THE FORCE
- **STAR WARS:** ICONS OF THE GALAXY
- **STAR WARS:** THE SAGA BEGINS
- **STAR WARS** THE ORIGINAL TRILOGY
- **STAR WARS:** ROGUES, SCOUNDRELS AND BOUNTY HUNTERS
- **STAR WARS:** CREATURES, ALIENS, AND DROIDS
- **STAR WARS: THE RISE OF SKYWALKER** THE OFFICIAL COLLECTOR'S EDITION
- **STAR WARS: THE MANDALORIAN:** GUIDE TO SEASON ONE
- **STAR WARS: THE EMPIRE STRIKES BACK** THE 40TH ANNIVERSARY SPECIAL EDITION
- **STAR WARS: AGE OF RESISTANCE** THE OFFICIAL COLLECTORS' EDITION
- **STAR WARS: THE SKYWALKER SAGA** THE OFFICIAL COLLECTOR'S EDITION
- **STAR WARS INSIDER: FICTION COLLECTION** VOLUME 1
- **STAR WARS INSIDER: FICTION COLLECTION** VOLUME 2

MARVEL STUDIOS LIBRARY

MOVIE SPECIALS
- **MARVEL STUDIOS'** *SPIDER-MAN FAR FROM HOME*
- **MARVEL STUDIOS'** *ANT-MAN AND THE WASP*
- **MARVEL STUDIOS'** *AVENGERS: ENDGAME*
- **MARVEL STUDIOS'** *AVENGERS: INFINITY WAR*
- **MARVEL STUDIOS'** *BLACK PANTHER* (COMPANION)
- **MARVEL STUDIOS'** *BLACK WIDOW*
- **MARVEL STUDIOS'** *CAPTAIN MARVEL*
- **MARVEL STUDIOS:** THE FIRST TEN YEARS
- **MARVEL STUDIOS'** *THOR: RAGNAROK*

marvel studios' avengers: an INSIDER'S guide TO THE AVENGERS' FILMS

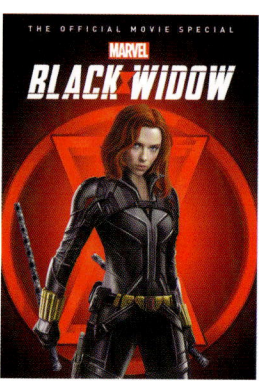
MARVEL STUDIOS' BLACK WIDOW The Official Movie Special

MARVEL STUDIOS' WandaVision THe official marvel studios collector special

MARVEL LEGACY LIBRARY

MARVEL CLASSIC NOVELS
- **WOLVERINE** WEAPON X OMNIBUS
- **SPIDER-MAN** THE DARKEST HOURS OMNIBUS
- **SPIDER-MAN** THE VENOM FACTOR OMNIBUS
- **X-MEN AND THE AVENGERS** GAMMA QUEST OMNIBUS
- **X-MEN** MUTANT EMPIRE OMNIBUS

NOVELS
- **SPIDER-MAN MILES MORALES** WINGS OF FURY
- **MORBIUS** THE LIVING VAMPIRE: BLOOD TIES
- **ANT-MAN** NATURAL ENEMY
- **AVENGERS** EVERYBODY WANTS TO RULE THE WORLD
- **AVENGERS** INFINITY
- **BLACK PANTHER** WHO IS THE BLACK PANTHER?
- **CAPTAIN AMERICA** DARK DESIGNS
- **CAPTAIN MARVEL** LIBERATION RUN
- **CIVIL WAR**
- **DEADPOOL** PAWS
- **SPIDER-MAN** FOREVER YOUNG
- **SPIDER-MAN** KRAVEN'S LAST HUNT
- **THANOS** DEATH SENTENCE
- **VENOM** LETHAL PROTECTOR
- **X-MEN** DAYS OF FUTURE PAST
- **X-MEN** THE DARK PHOENIX SAGA
- **SPIDER-MAN** HOSTILE TAKEOVER

ART BOOKS
- **MARVEL'S** *SPIDER-MAN MILES MORALES* THE ART OF THE GAME
- **MARVEL'S** *AVENGERS* THE ART OF THE GAME
- **MARVEL'S** *SPIDER-MAN* THE ART OF THE GAME
- **MARVEL** *CONTEST OF CHAMPIONS* THE ART OF THE BATTLEREALM
- **SPIDER-MAN: INTO THE SPIDER-VERSE:** THE ART OF THE MOVIE
- **THE ART OF IRON MAN** 10TH ANNIVERSARY EDITION

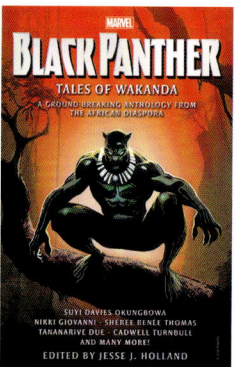
BLACK PANTHER TALES OF WAKANDA

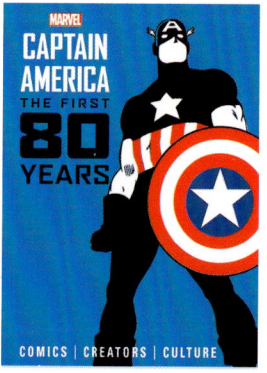
Marvel's Captain America: The First 80 Years

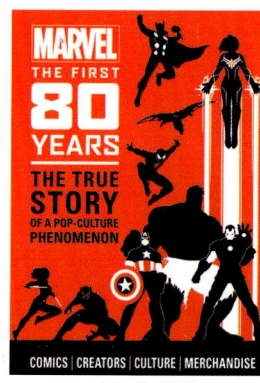
Marvel: The First 80 Years

AVAILABLE AT ALL GOOD BOOKSTORES AND ONLINE

titan-comics.com | titanbooks.com

© 2021 Lucasfilm Ltd. and ™. All Rights Reserved. Used Under Authorisation.
© 2021 MARVEL